Joy of MISSING Out

Niharika Nigam is from India and holds a Master's degree in the Science of Marketing from Manchester Business School, UK and has additionally studied Poetry writing and Social Entrepreneurship from the University of Oxford.

She is the Director Business Development of Jumpin Heights- the Bungy People and is the in-house self-appointed tester of all things adventure. She has Bungy Jumped a total of thirteen times so far and has published several articles on the power of standing on the edge in national media.

Joy of Missing Out

NIHARIKA NIGAM

NU VOICE PRESS

First published by NU VOICE PRESS 2024
An imprint of Hubhawks Pvt. Ltd
www.nuvoicepress.com

This is a work of fiction and all characters and incidents described in this book are the product of the author's imagination. Any resemblance to actual persons, living or dead, is entirely coincidental.

ISBN: 978-81-966888-7-5

Typeset by Saanvi Graphics, Noida
Printed at Thomson Press
Published by Nu Voice Press

To Papa,
For my wings.

To Mom,
For being the relentless wind underneath them.

Chapter 1

I have, I suppose, always been a closeted oddity. I've never *belonged* to the room, whichever one I'm in. But I bet you could never tell if you met me. Now, *that's* an art I've mastered over my thirty-one years of residing in this body, and I live the most regular life you can imagine. It is a standard template: How not to get caught? Blend in!

But that's not where my mastery lies. That's textbook for any version of an oddity not yet ready to be outed. My mastery lies in how I can shine even while staying concealed.

Hi, I'm Nanki Mehta, and in case you need to know, I identify as she/her, banal enough to coincide with my biological gender. Born into a middle-class family in a gated community near Qutub Minar, Delhi, I've lived, pretty much rooted like a tree, out of this very piece of earth for as long as I have existed. By some weird tryst of fate, even after I married Rithvik four years ago, it just so happened that instead of me moving out, he moved in with me, along with my grandfather, Nanu.

I don't hate it. Not this arrangement, not this colony, not this city. I am however certain that this heart is a vast thing because I have never seen it content within a small box, however much you may perfect it. The box, not the heart—that one remains hopelessly, thankfully untameable.

Maybe that's why I made the choices I did. During my college placement interviews, I met Jaya. She represented an unheard-of marketing firm in the country, and told me that I would get no pay for the first three months but would get to travel a lot. I took the job, and that became my career. What do you expect, trusting twenty-one-year-olds with those kinds of decisions? The job gave me what it promised, and I gave it my all. Anyway, ten years later, she's still my boss. It can only have been luck that Jaya went so much beyond that in my life. You'll see!

My parents, however, found another way to break through the monotony of 26 Geetanjali Enclave. A year after my wedding, they decided to relocate to Kodaikanal to live out their retirement plans, leaving me this property as a generous marital gift to settle into. Nanu, of course, had been too old to uproot and replant, so he came along with it by default. Now, he's my favourite souvenir of that feeling called 'home'.

It would have worked, you know. I could have stayed comfortably hidden in this perfectly average life.

But then this stupid world broke.

1.15 a.m.

I do one of two things at this hour. Ruminate over the day or scroll through Instagram. Right now, it seemed to be a bit of both.

Rithvik was already asleep, satisfied from having whipped up an excellent Tomato Pulao. I could hear Nanu cough through his sleep in the other room. Basically, the day had been as normal as can be right now, all things considered. Yet another lockdown was announced in the city, and we worked from home. Today was the fourth day I hadn't washed my hair, and it showed despite the messy bun that usually hid it well.

I was currently working on rebranding a sports beverage that aimed to 'give people just the energy boost they needed'. *As if.* No, there is nothing subtle about milking the cow of this ravaging sickness to increase sales. If it feels opportunistic and wrong, that's because it is. Yes, I'm aware of how I'm enabling this scam, but before you judge me, know that I have bills to pay, and morality isn't exactly affordable at the moment.

Having shared the drafts I knew were average, I wondered if my neighbour had found a hospital bed. Life, as we knew it, was crumbling down, and I was left trapped in it.

I pick up my phone after it beeps with a notification. Is it just me, or are we, as a generation, having our deepest conversations with Instagram now? I don't mean with our friends on the app. I mean *with* the app. Maybe, Instagram can hear our thoughts because it just threw up a post that was a direct response to my train of thought.

Can't wait to experience the world again?
We've got something you can hold onto!
Send us your story—why daring to take the last step off the edge is just what you need, and we'll gift you the experience of a lifetime:

INDIA'S MOST EXTREME BUNGY!
In Rishikesh!

Now *that* has my attention.

Chapter 2

I don't quite know whether I was half asleep or half awake, but I am up now. I picked up my phone, and this foreign-looking man with salty-looking hair, a dirty brown colour that curled carelessly at the edges, a mischievous twinkle in his eye, looked into the camera and out at me before edging towards jumping off what looked like a yellow bridge with ankle straps tied to a rubber cord. He raised his eyebrows, his eyes widened, and his face stretched as if to say 'eeeeeep… I can't believe I'm doing this!' He throws his arms out like a bird and bungy jumps; he looks so deliriously excited to be alive. That is an emotion I remember… and miss.

I rub my eyes, put on my earphones, and play it again.

And again.

With the sound on, I can now hear the wind gush wildly as a faint countdown erupts in the background: "3…2…1… JUMP!" right before his shrill shriek tears through, and he dives, full out, high on life.

I click on the post.

Can't wait to experience the world again?

I reread it thrice, and before I knew why, tears started to streak my face. It's like lightning and thunder these days. Emotions erupt with unexpected strength, and then the why makes itself heard. It probably always has been, but I never realised because it had been summer. Some events divide life into a before and an after. The pandemic had been waging for a year, with bad and then worse months. Far worse than anything anyone had anticipated. If I was out of place earlier, I was now fighting for just any place at all. But still. This had to be madness.

I mean, who cries at a Bungy advertisement? And yet, it feels cathartic.

I missed the world so much it hurt.

I miss the infectious energy of a crowd. I wish I had learnt how to become a part of it when I had the chance. I miss chasing the sun as Rithvik takes me on one of his endless drives with no destination. I miss the aunty I sat opposite every day on the metro. I miss travelling to new places and truly experiencing the world. It ached to see everything fall apart. I ached for my neighbour, for the people who died gasping for air, for togetherness. For health, for abundance. For the joy of being alive. For the warmth found in a cafe.

This was my life, my world, and it lay here now, just dying out. Silently tonight, I steal this moment to grieve. I grieve for the people I have never met and the places I have never been to. Most of all, I realise, I grieve for the time that was lost.

I click for details of this post, and it marks a location sticker: *Rishikesh!*

Ah, of course. I peer closer. The mountains behind the jumper, the sound of the wind... they transport me back.

You see, every family has that one place that ties their memories together. Where most summers were spent, where the fondest family pictures come from, where those anecdotes are born that become family legend. Rishikesh was that in ours: the place we went to to make enough happiness to last a year. Even after all these years, it felt familiar now. Mum would sit with her cup of chai by the Ganges, and Dad would love taking our pictures. Some days, we'd go rafting in the rapids of the Ganga and return home all wet from the chill waters of the holy river. And oh, the *pahadi khaana*—how much I miss it now! Cooked with locally-grown vegetables and sinfully greasy.

The warming camp bonfires were a comfortable memory, and I suddenly want to rewind (to that chapter)—but this time to think anew. I want to do everything I hadn't done here before. Be everyone I could have been. Build different from the same bricks.

Maybe then it might all end differently.

Maybe that's why that night I responded.

And that's how I met him.

Chapter 3

1.45 am

I want to consume those mountains and inhale them
until they fill me up
and nothing else remains.

I don't expect to hear back. No one responds to random Insta DMs anyway. I just wanted to *touch* Rishikesh, I guess. But within minutes, I see three dots light up and down. This random stranger, with clearly nothing better to do tonight, was responding!

You'd need an enormous appetite for that!
😉

Oops. There was a person on the other side of this phone.

Oh lol!
I meant I want to consume the mountains
like you do as you dive into them,
while I still have the chance
and while they still stand there,
unchanging and majestic.

I imagined him typing from the exact same spot as if he lived on that bungy bridge.

The messages weren't yet seen. I check his profile. It was the official page of the bungy place—Jumpin Heights. The bio read: *This is where you meet your fears. Got Guts?*

1 new notification

The stranger had responded with a picture. It was blurred for privacy's sake, and I wonder if I should open it. Oh well, it's a brand page. It couldn't be unsolicited pictures of the human anatomy. Or could it? I checked the time. It is almost 2 a.m. now. Got guts, eh? I take the risk, and carefully, suspiciously, I open it. It was a live picture, almost pitch black. In the distance, however, I could see the faint silhouette of the mountain ranges I know only too well: the Garhwali peaks at the foothills of the Himalayas. The mountains, right now.

Below it, he had written:

When this is all over,
they will be right here, waiting.
Unchanging and Majestic.

I stare at the picture. I take a deep breath and shut my eyes to burn the image in as if to lock it safely inside me. After a minute, I heart the picture because there really is nothing to say except, *"Pahaadon ki sardiyaan, aur kulhad waali chai. Bass, aur kya?"* Dad would have declared it as a life motto to a view like that. Remembering his deep, big voice now makes me feel safe and warm despite the chill in the air.

I zoom into the mountains again. If I look closely enough, I can almost hear them breathe.

Chapter 4

"Morning sunshiiiine!" Rithvik yells over my head while drawing the curtains. I try protesting in sleepy grunts at what I know is coming next. He hugs me before whispering, "Breakfast is your turn today!" With an evil laugh, he walks into his study.

I sit up on the bed and follow the light streaming in; both Rithvik and I had wanted a minimalist aesthetic, but this flat had seen three generations live here, and its eclecticism was a testimony to that. Dark wooden flooring with a white rug sprawled over it was our addition. The reading nook by the window was my grandparents' from two decades ago—Rithvik's favourite spot in the house. The cane study table across our bed was Mum's. An excess of big white fluffy comforters lay falling from our bed, and the room smelled like him. Musk.

As I reluctantly get out of bed, I knock over the photo frame resting on the bedside table. Our wedding photograph.

Rithvik and I never dated exactly. We were friends, and at some point, we decided to arrange our own marriage before our parents could do it for us. I'm as surprised as you are that I have a fully-functioning relationship. Don't get me wrong; I always had game. You'd be surprised at how much attention one can get by being disinterested in having it. Not to be cocky or anything, of course.

But a marriage is not just any relationship. It's the godfather of relationships.

I'm not averse to romantic love. I love it in fact—the fantasy of it. I know few who have known the real thing and lived to tell the tale, though. By that, I mean no one ever. But whatever this fluff is, the Bollywood way it is projected and expected to be, the way the *not* having it is romanticised too—it's cute in a nonsensical, consumable way. It just feels like something I see from the outside, if that makes sense. I still remember what Rithvik said when I told him that, throwing his head back, laughing, "Okay, but see what I find makes marriages the most romantic thing in the world, and yes, even today, is this: While in a relationship, when things go wrong, you question the other person, but in a marriage, if people go wrong, you question the institution. Whatever it is, it just is."

For that very reason, when this tall, beautiful, pepper-haired man, back from the US and working on a startup, asked me if I'd ever consider marrying him—I said yes.

And since then, it has just been. In a marriage like that, you don't fail because you don't expect fireworks. You expect the peace found in the dead of the night. You expect comfort. Offer valid till you have to make breakfast, apparently.

I half smile, half roll my eyes, and get out of bed to resume what seems like an endless day, broken only by a few naps and a couple of daydreams. It must've been around 10:45 a.m. when my phone rang only briefly after making *dosa* from store-bought batter with yesterday's sambar. I read Jaya's name flashing on the screen and immediately picked it up.

"Morning Jaya!"

"Ahaan. I've read your reports, Nanki. Why are you making a fool of me?"

My heart sinks, "Um … sorry?"

"This is not your best work, Nanki, and you know it."

Yup, I do. Oh God. You know when you're just doing enough at work to slide by unnoticed, and then that gets noticed? That is how I feel—caught at the scene of a crime, faking innocence.

"I'll redo it, Jaya. Sorry."

"Yes, you will," Jaya responds, in that curt voice I hate. Then, mercifully, she adds, "Get it together, kiddo."

"One hundred per cent. Sorry again." I hang up.

This stings because I remember Jaya applauding me at our Gurugram office not that long ago after yet another winning pitch. "My go big or go home kind of girl," she had said.

Oh, I had always loved bringing brands to life. I brought to my design what I kept hidden in my relationships: I allowed myself to be bold and audacious. Dangerous almost, for the thrill of having it seen. Nobody could be me at our swanky Cyberhub office, and Jaya made sure I knew that. She made sure the whole office knew that, which is also why I have no friends from work. Over the last decade, she has entrusted me with brands that were willing to step outside the box or at least who could be nudged into it.

In turn, I would take their mere retail products and weave them into a story that would magically fit right into the world you live in. No, the world you *want* to live in. Whoever you are, you will come seeking this product because your reality is better with the fantasy I'm baking it into at the Layman and Associates headquarters.

That whacko personality is what landed me this project.

But of late, I can't even find it.

"Found anything yet?"

Rithvik pops into the room and asks. He's asking for Kavya, our twenty-year-old neighbour, who had not yet found a hospital bed for her mother in need of a ventilator. I give him a death stare. I haven't found a thing because I haven't been looking. Where I am, only PowerPoint and Zoom meetings live.

Dismissing my resistance, he adds: "I think her dad has Viral-X, too. He's been showing symptoms."

Uff. I shut my eyes for a brief second before I yell into my computer:

"Jeff, it's nine p.m."

"So? It's not like you have to be at the office. Besides, it's eleven-thirty here. We're not complaining, are we?" Jeff from our Singapore office is leading with me on this account. Kinda against me, but butting heads is encouraged in modern-day work ethic, so whatever. This beverage company is trying to relaunch an orange drink in the South-Asian market within the next quarter. They were desperate, which meant huge marketing budgets and a handsome profit for the company. It's sort of become Singapore vs India at this point. He was exhausting in general but had never been this uncouth. I want to punch him in the face. I do. Instead, I visibly roll my eyes, contain my curses, and reply, "I'll send over the new theme options by midnight," and bang my laptop shut.

Urgh, adulting.

2 a.m.

"Mails sent. Twitter refreshed every minute. Telegram groups stalked. Nothing. Just nothing, anywhere," I tell Rithvik, who's been doing the same routine next to me.

He keeps his phone aside and props himself up on one elbow to look at me.

"We'll try again tomorrow. How was your day otherwise?"

I want to answer but am too tired to relive the details.

"Regular," I say and sink into my comforter, finally.

He begins to say something, then doesn't. Before rolling over, he adds, "Oh, chai is over. Tell the *kirana* to deliver it tomorrow."

"Tch. Should have told me earlier, no."

Now tomorrow morning, everyone will go without chai, and I'll have to live with the guilt of it. As I wait for sleep, I think about the day I had agreed to marry Rithvik when he asked. I remember it so clearly: it was because he let silence exist between us. This is not to say we don't have anything to say: We can talk for days about things that don't matter, and you'd be surprised at how many marriages hinge well enough on just that. It is just that I'm used to being my own processing unit about things that *do*. With him, I could stay unseen, safely tucked inside, and he seemed to like me anyway without forcing my doors open. That, to me, was a promise of safety.

Within this confinement, however, I am beginning to see the promise falter. Maybe it's because he misses his friends. He has always been so social. Or maybe it is because he is stuck with me, without anyone else to talk to now. Or maybe he thought all along that I'd change someday.

Something Jaya used to teach me haunts me now:

Every relationship can be a success if you know what distance to keep it at.

And right now, we could afford none.

Chapter 5

The next couple of days came in like a hurricane. Kavya had not yet found a bed for her mother when her father was diagnosed as Viral-X-positive too and declared critical. This was a bad movie script playing out in real life. Little Kavya. She was barely out of her teens and the older of two siblings. At a time when neighbours had no reason to talk to each other, hers was the only family on the street we actually had a relationship with. They were the only ones we sent Diwali sweets over to share food with.

As I find myself assimilating the Jenga blocks of our relationship as if to brace for impact, I realise how exquisitely rudimentary it was, like the most basic of human instincts, and yet—or maybe that is why—it was my only sense of community amidst this otherwise concrete jungle. Can you imagine an entire familial unit breaking down? I wouldn't wish it upon anyone, but least of all them.

Little Kavya, who had run to the medical store to get me medicines during a viral when Rithvik was travelling on work. She had got me an extra pack of chocolate biscuits that day, just because I only ever have orange-cream biscuits, but

Kavya didn't know that. So she bought me the best thing she could from the store—her own favourite flavour. Somehow, I loved that even more. Kavya always saved me a piece of her birthday cake, even when I was too busy to attend. Again, always chocolate. Little Kavya, not being allowed to be so little anymore.

No. I stopped my train of thought before it started to make room for the worst. What if I invite misery in? Isn't that The Secret or Law of Attraction or whatever?

But then, we're probably all just doomed.

With all the papers, the social media, and the news, there was no escaping the fear. If the fear set in, there was no escaping the possibility of... So no, I am not going to think it. Let's just find a bed for now.

Rithvik was on a call with yet another hospital. His father was a renowned surgeon, and we were trying to pull all the strings possible.

No vacancy.

I was sitting at the edge of my seat, barely able to eat. Jeff was texting me furiously, insisting I join the conference call with the client in an hour.

They had just collated some data from their recent sales in the Middle East and wanted to highlight their estimated causes for the 7% jump in sales there.

I could not care less. Not a wee bit—minus one.

This was so ridiculously unimportant that right at this moment, I didn't care if I was unemployed for the rest of my life. I let his calls ring out and wonder what would happen if I just ghosted him and the rest of the company forever, starting now. I pick up the phone for no reason again and realise that I can't even put the phone on silent. What if a hospital or lead got back with a vacancy?

As Rithvik is making call after call, I keep refreshing the local hospital databases on Twitter and Telegram for absolutely any relief. I had put out urgent requests everywhere. So many people responded to requests, with such a barrage of information, that just sent me down one wild goose chase after another, all leading to nowhere. All unverified and outdated sources.

My phone rings. I jerk towards it, hoping to hear from one of the doctors. It was Jaya. I roll my eyes.

"JEFF, that RAT!" I mutter malevolently. Complaining to the headmistress like we're in school! Absolute worst of humanity, scum of the earth.

He knew I would never leave Jaya hanging, and that's why he played this card.

"Hello." I take a deep breath in to calm myself down.

"Nanki, you've been unavailable. You're needed in the meeting in twenty minutes."

Jaya was the human version of an official text.

After a deliberately audible sigh, I purse my lips, nod my head in resignation and say, "Yes, Jaya."

"Good girl!" she responded, with a hint of warmth that dripped slowly like golden honey and, in doing so, made it even more precious. Her way of conveying a virtual hug, without indulging my issues, as if already knowing of them and yet nudging me onward to plough through anyway, as if to say, 'March on, soldier'.

And I did. I respected her too much to refuse.

It's instances like these I'm sure why my colleagues made jokes about Jaya being my work mom. Simple, stout, and formidable, late-fifty-something Jaya. In her crisp cotton sari and big red bindi, Jaya had recruited me right out of college as a lanky third-year student with my hair streaked red and the white canvas sports shoes that were all the rage in Delhi University at the time. She had mentored me into becoming the professional I am today (read: usually) and the person I had come to be.

My parents, I'm sure, were relieved too. They had been burdened with way too much for way too long anyway, what with the grief of losing their first child, two years before I was born, at six months old. A grief that I never actually experienced, but that somehow became like the unseeable air around me. They pretended they were complete with just me, and I pretended to believe them. They pretended that I could fill the void she left behind, and I pretended to believe them. I hid myself away to project the illusion of who she might be, and I kept chasing this ghost of a person, this fantasy, and we all pretended like it worked. In the pretence of it all, I forgot how to not pretend with people. Or how to let them in.

So when Jaya walked in and offered me an identity I could grow into, it pretty much saved my life. In investing in polishing me, standing behind me, and pushing me forward, Jaya gifted me an inherent sense of confidence and self-esteem. For that, I would forever be indebted. And so, I found a way to accommodate this one meeting into my otherwise nerve-wracking day, concealing my anxiety under a peach lipstick and a careless swipe of kohl.

Rithvik's phone rang at three a.m. I awoke with a startle. I don't know if it was a dream or the uneasiness of the day, but my heart was racing.

This happened often as a knee-jerk reaction to alarms these days.

Rithvik jerked out of his blanket, fumbling to reach his mobile. Sitting up straight, he put on his glasses as if his sight was imperative to this conversation.

"H-Hello ... ? Ahaan ... ? Okay ... okay!" He reached for a notepad and scribbled something down.

"Thank you so much, sir ... thank you."

His voice was still so full of sleep, but he was excited as he hung up.

"Nanki, they have one oxygen concentrator system. Ready to be delivered. They'll set up a unit at home. Just have to email the postal address; I'm doing it now. You call Kavya."

The call had been from one of the foundations we had called earlier in the day.

I dialled Kavya. She picked up so fast, like she regularly spent her nights attached to her phone, waiting for it to ring.

"Hi, didi?"

The question mark at the end of her hello would echo in my ears for a long time to come. She was waiting for us to get help. No, not just waiting, asking for a miracle we had no power to deliver. Like a child must look to God in prayer. I thanked my stars, for I did have some good news to give tonight, but I was not prepared for what followed.

"We have one ventilator. They are coming home to set it up. Rithvik is getting ready, and he will handle it. Just stay up."

Kavya burst into tears. She kept mumbling something amidst a thousand thank yous.

"Kavya? It's going to be okay," I say, but it feels empty, even to me. 'Okay' was a luxury now, and I had no authority to make such claims.

"Didi, should I give it to Mom or Dad?"

Chapter 6

"You can never do that to us! We would die if it were not for you. When you were born, the panditji said you've come to heal us—as our blessing. Everything we do, we do for you. We only want your happiness. Without that, what is the point of anything? You can never, ever be sad. I would have failed at everything otherwise," my mum clung on to this existence with a thin thread. I remember her shaking.

I don't know why this is a core memory. It was a fairly regular narrative around our household. This was somewhere between my mid-teens; I had tried throwing a tantrum for something I can't quite remember anymore, and my mum had flown off the handle in a fit of tears. I wished with all my heart that, for once, she'd meet me with anger instead of disintegrating entirely.

She was pleading for me to be happy… to be perfect.

Restlessness is painful to watch. Some people have souls that jangle inside the shell of their body caged. Trapped with a void that has nowhere to go; restless for something lost a long time ago—that was my mother, since always. With a wispy frame and greying hair, she existed like she was merely tolerating the ordeal of living. If you saw her, you'd think she functioned fine. You'd think that of all of us.

Tantrums were rare for me to begin with. I had learned early on that there was too much on everyone's plate, what with digesting the ghost of my sister and hoping I'd be the soul of the daughter they lost—perfect in their fantasy. I mostly felt like a fraud living her life, an imposter guest in my own home.

Mum wiped the tears off her face, held me close, shivering and somehow, like always, I consoled her instead. "I'm the luckiest girl in the world," I said, "and I'm very happy."

And I stayed that way. Very, very happy, till I couldn't be anything else with anyone else anymore. Very, very happy till it suffocated the life out of me.

Meh, better me than them. Besides, for them, I'd suffocate a million times over.

"D-didi? Mom or Dad?" Kavya repeats. I come out of my reverie and into this moment.

There is a long pause, the kind there is when a patient flatlines. I feel a despair so absolute that I feel as though all hope is lost. How could I answer that question? How could I protect Kavya from having to make that choice? There was no way out. I wish I could protect her from what was to come, but this had to be done. Holding tears back, I ask, "What do you think?"

"Okay, so mum, of course, needed it first, but I th-think we may be too far deep to save her," her voice cracked. It was probably the first time she was admitting this, even to herself. The tears refused to obey any longer and rolled down my face.

"If we don't get another ventilator soon, I don't want Dad to..." her voice trailed off.

This was supposed to have been *good* news. All words seemed to have left my vocabulary.

"Does this m-mean I'm letting mum die? Am I really letting my mother die?" Little Kavya was getting her words out through haunting wails now. She was all broken. I will never forgive myself for the words I should have said, but that never came to me. Maybe they just did not exist. There is a certain melancholy so deep that 'cry' is just too darn small for it. On that cold winter night, as I held onto my phone, I wept.

A van drove into our locality. You don't see stars in the Delhi night sky, so there isn't much to look for there anyway. While I nervously paced my balcony, my eyes stayed glued to the road, desperate to see the help that was promised to drive in. A couple of men wearing the whole nine yards of protective gear* got out. I had seen it on TV, but in person, it looked like a scene from a sci-fi movie about to segway into horror. Imagine four men, masked from head to toe, inside plastic garb getting out of a van in the dead of night in a regular residential colony, and we feel... relief. Weird, weird time. Anyway, as I peer closer, I see them holding a big carton. Perching it carefully between them, they walk into Kavya's building. The urgency in their stride allows such intense relief to wash over me that my knees almost buckle.

"I think the oxygen concentrator has arrived! Rith-Rithvik?" I look behind me, thinking he's in the connecting living room. Empty.

"On it!" He yells from the kitchen, making chai, I'm sure.

He scurries out, hands me a steaming mug, and rushes out toward the lift.

"Mask!" I bark. He steps back and picks one up from the foyer.

I look back down.

Rithvik waits by Kavya's gate to handle the paperwork afterwards. I look closer at the van and read the bright hand-painted art sprawled across it:

Dharma Foundation
Oxygen Langar #OnWheels

I bring my phone out and do a quick Google search. A very basic website reveals a group of turbaned men running this charity full-time for a decade. In the Sikh community, a langar was traditionally a free communal kitchen attached to their temple or Gurdwara. Living in North India meant being well acquainted with Sikhism. Although meant for the hungry, the langar was usually so rich in flavour and love—that it attracted tourists, students, and the well-fed alike, and no one was ever turned away.

Seva or service was an integral aspect of their faith, which meant to help the community without expectations or returns. Towards that altruistic end, during the pandemic, I gathered from the website this organisation had taken their communal distribution drive to the roads to arrange for oxygen to those who were starving of breath.

Chai in hand, I ruminate over this, all sleep having left my system as day and night merged into one ambiguous hue of restlessness.

To serve for services' sake: the simplest, kindest, and most extraordinary of motives. No exchange is needed because you can—no, actually, because you *get* to.

About forty-five minutes passed before the men emerged from the building and huddled around Rithvik below, leaving a distance of about 6 feet, discussing something in hushed tones. One of the men looked up, and for a fleeting second, our eyes locked.

Maybe I'm high on exhaustion and chai fumes, but even though he was a fair distance away and partially hidden behind the face shield, I swear I saw this *something* in his eyes: like ... like ... *purpose*. On fire. Not the kind that erupts into flames, consuming everything in sight before dying out, but another distinctive kind—one that is silent, rebellious, and resolute. The kind that perseveres. A fire that sparked an ember within me.

As he looks away, I feel so terribly small in comparison. It is a strange ordeal to watch what must be God in motion. I had no idea it could look like this: being star-struck by this most ordinary man, acting out the simplest of teachings: to just do good. And look at what that did—it allowed someone to breathe another day. So, simplicity, if done right, is enough. Why is no one teaching us that? I mean, look at us. He and I are seemingly cut from the same fabric and woven of the same threads, and yet, he is infinitely more than I have ever been.

Once Rithvik was done with the formalities, the men moved swiftly back into their van, onwards towards probably saving another. I feel a pang of envy at their sheer movement. What a privilege it must be to give and feed and provide, and the blessing was truly the givers'—they got to justify their existence as an integral link in the invisible chain that connects us all.

As I watch them drive into the sunrise, I am consumed by a singular thought:

It must be terrifying to wear this much worth. But for the first time ever, I wanted to know it for myself.

Even as one continued to gasp for air, we had just been thrown a lifeboat for another, and it was time to grab on tight.

Not knowing what to do next, I let that ember guide me, and it took me into the most surprising of places: my kitchen.

Although a first for me, I only did what people must have done since the beginning of time for each other from love. As a show of the first gesture of solidarity ever known to mankind, what neighbourhoods and communities must have been built upon:

I took over some freshly prepared, piping hot food for the family next door.

Chapter 7

Like the cold that is left behind after the fog has lifted, a peculiar disquiet had settled into my bones by nighttime, worming its way deeper into the centre of my chest. I seemed to be wrapped in a thick blanket of icy air. Although I was breathing, it was uncomfortable. Not for any sickness; I was quite well, thank you very much. The discomfort now was simply the ordeal of being alive amidst death. How do you state that out loud when even that was such a luxury to have? A luxury people were scrounging, tugging, and dying for? You don't. You bow your head, say thank you to whatever power keeps you alive, and breathe through it all. But I seriously doubt if it would ever entirely leave me now. Much as ivy takes hold of trees, this too was becoming part of my being, feeding on me, breathing with me, and growing along with me.

Rithvik was already asleep. Even though it was technically his turn in the kitchen today, I took it up because he deserves the rest. I look at his head barely out of the comforter, and I hope he knows I'm grateful to have him around.

Attachments are tricky for me, and only because I never had much need for them. I have operated alone, and well enough, might I add, for far too long and for far too much to have the bone to accommodate another entity with all their feelings and all that neediness. The reason we worked this long is because Rithvik's neediness is, in fact, so high it makes up for the lack of mine. I mean moulds-himself-around-the-space-I-need much. I have always suspected lingering abandonment issues from his childhood, but whatever makes him *him,* this man, on my worst day, would never leave me, of that, I'm sure. I guess that makes us a modern-day fairytale.

Oh, don't go picking me apart. I made him rajma chawal too, didn't I? That is pretty much what love looks like after the first five hundred days of entanglement. Well, what can I say? It does take chaotic days sometimes to appreciate having someone to handle the mess.

I yawn and look away. I pick my phone up, escaping into the world of social updates. Other people's lives make for a better view right now. Today had been what one might think of as a good day, all things considered. I think of how Kavya is doing and feel empty inside. If only I could legit climb outside of my body and be anywhere but here.

Anywhere but here. I suddenly remember something. But my fingers seemed to have beaten me to it. Before I know it, I'm already scrolling through my DMs to get to him.

11:25 p.m.

I know this might be weird, but you've done this before,
and it meant so much then,
and if it's possible, it would mean even more today.
So, if it isn't too much to ask for,
can you please just take me to Rishikesh tonight?

Nothing to lose here, right? Of course, he might never respond. Or he just might.

Until I know for sure, I can stay comfortably suspended in the hope that Rishikesh might just be 'out for delivery'. That was enough to soothe me through this minute. And the next twenty. I didn't even care about the outcome by the time my phone vibrated with a new notification.

'Tap to see blurred content', Instagram announced. This time, unhesitatingly, I clicked on it as soon as it arrived in my inbox. A burst of colour takes over my screen. Rushes of vivid imagery in quick succession make my head spin momentarily. I pause it, tuck a stray strand of hair behind my ear and give my brain a second to pick up speed to grasp better. It was a live video shot from atop a bike as the rider zipped through the bazaar in the heart of Rishikesh. I catch dizzying glimpses as rushes of the narrow, bustling street fly by.

Vegetable hawkers, people in colourful sweaters and a few in orange robes, fairy lights and bulbs lighting up the road, Rudraksha beads hanging from every other stall, tall posters of various Gods encased in gaudy gold fabric with tassels almost leaping out of them, and despite the loud VRROOMM of the revving engine, the trance-devotional music permeating everything like a heartbeat.

Ah. I take a deep breath as if to inhale Rishikesh.

From years of visits, I could tell where this was—just a turn away from Lakshman Jhula, the suspension bridge across the wild Ganges. Despite myself, I could feel my tired face crack into a smile. Jumping up and down over the Lakshman Jhula as a child is probably one of my favourite memories. Such random scraps of memory fill me up now, like an echo reaching out from safer times. Mum feeding chana to the monkeys nearby, and Dad reprimands her for it. Laughter. I remember a lot of laughter as I jumped as high as I could, hoping to buoy over the current of air that apparently made the bridge move to its own special rhythm. Maybe I felt it only because I tried so hard to, but I didn't care. Abandoning all caution like the Ganga below me, Lakshman Jhula and I just flowed in perfect harmony, as if a part of some grand orchestra.

This stranger had just gifted me a little pocket of comfort. That's what I needed; a little flight of fancy. Looking at this video now mentally transported me to a safer land away from the confines of this bed, no questions asked. I was beyond grateful, for I had neither the energy nor the words to explain the why. Service for services' sake. I ended the day with what I started it on.

Thank you, stranger. Above and beyond.

I hesitated, then typed:

Also, what's your name?

You're very welcome.

I don't know what you are going through, but it's the least I can do.

Bring you a piece of my world—or maybe just a piece of yours back to you.

And hi there! I'm River.

River! I mouth the word till I feel it play on my lips, sitting just right like the perfect note in a melody. I could not believe I had gone without knowing a name like that my entire life. But it was here now. As a brand strategist, it is my whole job to find words, names, and ideas that evoke. Most human names evoke images; his, however, brought up sounds—of gurgling, abundant, pristine water. Just flowing effortlessly, giving life along the way, nourishing everything it touched. I turn my unnecessary brainstorming off and remind myself—he's not my project. If anything, I am his.

Maybe on another day, I might have assumed this to be a fake identity. God knows there's no shortage of that online. But something about this felt right, almost perfect. How do you feel familiar with something you have never known before? Oh well, maybe it's just exhaustion after all.

River. What a beautiful, beautiful name.

Why aren't more people called River?
Why isn't everybody?

I need sleep. But I had just about found an exit route from my nightmare, and I wasn't ready to give it up just yet.

Hahaha, then I'm not sure anyone would want it anymore.

Humans have a way of wanting what they don't have.
We are quite the odd lot, aren't we?

That we are.

Makes one wonder

if what keeps us ticking is simply our constant yearning.

What a nightmare it would be then,
to have all that we desire.

I have no bandwidth left for random wonderments about existence. I was barely getting by on my own. I had felt and thunk my whole quota for the day today, maybe the year to be honest. So, forgive me for wanting to splash around the surface.

A bungy jumper who's also a philosopher?

That must be new.

Nah, I am not a philosopher. Just a liver.

As innn... the organ?

Oops, hahah... no! A LIVER. Of life.

Is that not a word?

Trust Instagram to get weird in 0.01 seconds. Where did this guy come from? At this point, it might as well have been Pluto.

Ummmmmm

No?

Oh?

How come? It should be!
We need a word for someone who is just being alive,
like proactively...
A LIVER!!

Kinda starting to feel like I'm talking to an alien. 😛

I'm sorry, English is not my first language.
I find it hard to connect the dots sometimes.

I read his chat again. Half smiling, I have the inkling that he was going to be wrong about this one.

What a shame, though. The language loses out.

Indeed, it does.

He was right. I suddenly felt hurt at how right he was. How very incomplete all the dictionaries of the world have been without this word—or a word for this. Any word that did not sound like an organ!

Where are you from?

I come from France.

And I am the Bungy Jump Master here.

Whoa. He clearly didn't have to deal with the Jeffs of the world.

I thought it only qualifies as a French name if the rest of us just have to butcher the Rs and Hs and everything in between.

Hahahhahahhahahah which is why I chose this name for 'the rest of you'.

That's a lot of hahahas. Giggly guy! Also, chose this name.

The plot thickens. I would have found that ridiculous had I not had enough experience working with our Singapore office, where they adopt English names for 'the rest of us'. I don't ask his real name—feels invasive somehow.

So you sell excitement for a living.

No wonder you've taken up the cause of THE LIVER
for the English language...

as you have in life.

Gawd! He calls himself River. He is a Bungy Jump Master in the foothills of the Himalayas. He throws people off the edge for money. He unknowingly saves the day by sending random people on the internet a virtual tour of Rishikesh.

To think what life could also look like on some people. Either this is entirely crazy or wholly beautiful. Maybe that's eventually the same thing.

I guess I do!

But WHY I do it is because people seem to forget that:
That this is it! This is life.

The edge reminds them of that. And me.
Every. Single. Day.

And if this is all there is,
Then what else is there to do with life than to live it,
all too completely?

Ah…

A liver.

I see it now.

I am keenly aware that he had not yet asked for my name. By this point, others would be enquiring about one's relationship status, so you understand when I say that this makes me trust him.

I'm Nanki, btw. Good night, River :)

My eyes were screaming for sleep.

Good night, Nanki.

🌠

My body now refused to function anymore, and I let myself surrender to the night. As one last thing, though, I hit the 'follow' button before switching off.

Chapter 8

Okay, I'm processing it now. Nanu sat reading his newspaper on the futon, his chai by his side, and his trusty Caravan playing Shekhar Ravjiani's Hanuman Chalisa that filled my morning with a 'detoxification' that came along with a catchy tune. I'm standing in my balcony, already cramped with just three potted plants, and look out at the street below. Mahesh, the grocer's teenage son from down the street, had come to deliver the week's supplies to the building as per telephonic orders. Every Friday, he would leave it down below, outside the gate of the building, to be picked up individually for a contactless delivery. I had given him a standing order to add a pack of chocolates to Kavya's basket every week.

Kavya's mother had passed away two days after her dad had received the oxygen concentrator. What was most devastating was that by that point, it had come as a relief. Her father, on the other hand, was doing better. There was no telling how Kavya was doing. Well, she was surviving. It was as little and as much as that.

"*Bete*, aaya?"

Nanu calls from the living room, eagerly waiting for the Parle-G, which we had run out of last evening. He had not touched his cup of tea in the absence of its partner.

I spot three packs in our basket. "*Aa gaya*!" I peek in to tell him. He gives me a toothy grin, relieved and breaks into song as he bobs his head to "*Jai Siyaram, Jai Siyaram.*"

A Liver, I think to myself and shake my head, laughing at the theatrics, and say, "Why are you troubling Ramji for what *apna* Mahesh can do?"

"Ramji says, therefore Mahesh does!" he says with a flair. Folding his legs up, he holds out his mug to me and requests childlike, "*Jaa, le aa.*"

I rush down.

Anand Grocery was a rudimentary store supplying my childhood indulgences for as long as I could remember. Now, as our gated colony of buildings stayed locked down on account of the Viral-X patients, including Kavya's father, it was reduced to a cold transactional supplier of rations. So much of the joy of purchasing was leaning across the counter to look at the goodies stacked up to the ceiling like Alice in Wonderland. At Lalaji's welcoming smile and insistence on pushing the week's special offers while asking how Nanu was keeping. In sliding in the sour candy he knew I loved instead of the last few coins of the change. But it was more than that.

So much of my sense of abundance came from knowing that it stayed lit-up every day of the week, just around the corner, never running out. I never realised that then of course. Only now, in its absence, as I pick up this jute bag of our week's rations.

River's words echo in my mind: "It's the least I can do. Bring you a piece of my world—or maybe just a piece of yours back to you."

A piece of yours back to you.

Yes. Somehow, being confined to my own home felt like being caged in. That must mean ... that so much of me lay outside of me.

If I feel so much lesser by being separated from it, it must mean that I *belonged* to the world.

A beautiful, beautiful world that I never even realised how much I was a part of till I couldn't be anymore. It was like a symbiotic relationship in itself—my internal ecosystem and the world outside. There could be no harmony in one when there was chaos raging in another. A very codependent relationship, it seems to be too ... Either that or my sense of belonging lies like a lost locket somewhere outside entirely.

As I enter the house again, my train of thought is halted as I see Nanu coughing violently from the living room. Rithvik keeps insisting we should get him tested, and I can hear him nag inside my head every time I hear that cough. I've been waiting for it to pass as these colds normally do. It hasn't so far.

His chai would've gotten cold by now. I drummed my fingers on the doorway in frustration and walked straight into the kitchen to make him a hot cup of ginger tea. I can't have him go through this. Stupid, *stupid* cold, worrying everyone for no reason. Why isn't it going away already?

Rithvik had suggested isolating him for a couple of days. I had refused. He was old, and he needed me. And I needed him. Rithvik cared so much about Nanu that it was annoying.

Mostly because I felt obliged to accommodate his concern for him as if his love carried more weight. In India, women rarely got to prioritise their maiden families after marriage the way I did. If they were lucky, they got to bring along their individuality—but any baggage, like the family, was casually expected to be left behind, only to be visited once in a while, as guests do. If they did even that too often or stayed too long, the marriage's stability was quickly put under the scanner for viruses. A precarious balance needed to be maintained so that the neighbours didn't have too much to talk about as they dipped their glucose biscuits into their cups of tea. That seemed to be an integral factor in all of decision-making.

Bagging a man open to inviting his wife's kin into his everyday life and loving them as his own was then seen as nothing lesser than a wish upon a falling star. This made Rithvik a frikkin' unicorn. Despite my feminist leanings, I hated that I felt grateful. As I added two spoonfuls of tea leaves into the pot of boiling water, Rithvik walked in, almost at a trot.

"Nanki, seriously, man, do you hear him? We have to get the test done . . . ."

His voice trailed off as he caught me glaring at him through the fumes from the bubbling tea.

A frown sprouted up on his face as his worried expression transitioned into a quizzical look comically fast, wondering what he did wrong.

"Fine," I said rather curtly before pouring all the tea into mine and Nanu's cup, leaving him standing alone to make his own.

Chapter 9

Now for the rest of the day, it was going to niggle at the back of my head. The front was occupied by a series of meetings, which, as tiresome as they were, kept me from obsessing over Nanu's test reports. It was the day after the conversation. A man in a white lab coat had come home in the morning wearing a mask and a face shield to do the swab test. He explained that he would put an earbud up Nanu's nose and another around his mouth before proceeding to do it.

Nanu was a champ. He listened to him, offered him water, glanced at me, and laughed as if to say, "Well if these are the ways of this new world…"

The man opened a plastic bag with fresh, sanitised supplies and proceeded with his test. One earbud was clinically thrust up his nose, far too deep for comfort, making him retch.

"*Arre, arre*?" I glared at him. I could very well have been a ghost because he didn't so much as bat an eyelid. Rithvik held me back, and I whispered to him, "Can they not be gentler?" He purses his lips and gestures to me to wait. The other earbud was swirled around his mouth to collect saliva and was done in a jiffy. Nanu looked up at us and smiled, putting up his palms to tell us he was okay. He was trying to calm us down. He was eighty-seven, which meant this could go wrong a thousand ways.

I decided to think about the handful of ways it could be okay. Maybe it was just a regular viral. They do still exist, after all. Nanu decided to be in his room in self-isolation today but kept his door open. Neither here nor there, but caught in just a little bit of limbo. I made him a flask of tea and let my meetings take over. Today, Jaya was leading the discussions on a Zoom video call.

"So, as you see, we need to shift our target audience from teenagers to the late twenties and early thirties bracket. Increasing our price point will help us achieve that. It may sound counter-intuitive now, but there's a better chance of survival by completely rebranding than rehashing the old product in just prettier packaging."

Jeff interjected, "However, we need to consider how people would take to a new drink at a higher price in times of a recession when the economy is already reeling. Beverages are not a necessity, and a crisis of this scale, in fact, deems it as a luxury..."

What if the report comes back positive? My brain had this other tab open that seemed to have frozen, persistently lit up in the background.

In the meeting, however, there were two rounds of back and forth before someone asked me pointedly, "Nanki, what's your take?"

You really can't get away with *zombie-ing* your team, mid-meeting, can you? Zombie-ing is a term that Kavya had taught me about the current dating scene, one where someone thinks they can ghost you and come back like nothing happened. Oh, I feel old.

"Um, yeah, I think we need to rope in the client to see how they feel about it because it is a big decision. Of course, this wouldn't change the product, just our brand communication around it...."

My voice drifted as another idea seemed to have suddenly birthed itself inside me.

"Wait..." I start slowly, stealing a moment to gather my thoughts. "Why don't we market it as a necessity though? Take it down from the luxury beverages category and sell it as an essential lifestyle product towards an energy boost, subtly hinting at mental health fatigue around the pandemic. If it works, we get to capitalise on the spending power of the working population while not losing out on the budget buyer." There was a silence while everyone mulled this over. I felt sick to my stomach.

"This.... will require very careful planning and execution. If done right, it will be a game changer for this brand," Jeff delivered the verdict carefully.

Jaya seemed tense, "We must get the client in the loop as soon as we have a basic strategy in place."

For two hours after that, they discussed the various ways they could position the brand in this unique way. Somewhere deep inside my body, that tab was still open, and it was still glitching. My heart would start racing every time I thought about what if... What if it is positive? Between a couple of 'hmms' and 'yesses', my mind kept buzzing with a pulsating fear. Would he be able to make it through this if it is?

Rithvik walked in, tiptoeing around me since yesterday. "*Oyi,* do you want to take lunch to Nanu?"

I looked up from my laptop and wondered why he couldn't just do it.

"Erm, meeting?" I answer like I'm teaching a monkey the basics of being human. Another member from our Delhi office and another from Singapore were bickering over the budget for one of the marketing campaigns.

He gives me a dirt eye, finally irritated by my moods. Shaking his head, he mouths 'fine' before leaving the room.

See, I need to be doing well here because outside this tiny little space was a world of uncertainty. That was tougher to deal with. It's fine if he doesn't get it. It's fine if you don't either. I just wanted to run so hard from there that I think I may have caught some speed. An odd energy seemed to have taken charge of me today. Like a woman possessed, I was flying with it.

"….And if the client doesn't mind altering the product composition ever so slightly," I cut in, interrupting Maria's pitch of a hypothetical ad campaign, "we could add a dash of turmeric and say it improves immunity."

There was a pause as everyone absorbed this. I knew—oh, I just knew that this idea was a winner. The drink was a tropical, orange energy drink. A tiny amount of turmeric would alter neither the colour nor the taste of the drink—but could potentially change their entire brand communication and, thereby, perception.

My brain was on *fire* today. I didn't know what was spurring me on, but it felt electric. I think I got my mojo back.

"Oh my god, yes!" Jeff's low whisper failed to mask his excitement. "The exotically traditional punch to resonate with the urban Indian market. The magical cure to all health ailments—Turmeric! Genius!" His admiration made my skin crawl. I could hear Nanu cough in the other room. I suppressed a pang of *something.* Something that was new inside me. On the one hand, I was finally being myself, doing my thing, and acting exactly as I was designed to be.

And on the other, this softer voice was emerging, meeker—almost like a baby trying to make itself heard. I could tell this voice apart by how it repulsed away from my own. I know I need to make sense of it, but I'm suddenly drowning as the screen erupts in a brand new cacophony, excited at what this proposition could mean. I sit back, a niggling thought forming at the back of my mind. Somehow, the room within has become too small for my own being.

I don't know what time it is anymore, but I feel hungry. It must be around dinner since the sun had set a long while ago, and as I stretch my hands in front of me, Rithvik runs in, looking deathly pale. The hair at the back of my neck stands for some reason.

"Nanu's reports just came in."

My stomach lurches. I think I knew what was coming before he said it.

"He's got Viral-X."

Chapter 10

So much of what came after that was a blur. I remember not being able to move. Rithvik's words echoed inside my head while I tried to grasp what had just happened.

How could it be? How was this even possible?

My meeting was still dragging on, suddenly in an alternate universe. I jerked out of bed and left without warning, leaving my laptop open, my screen staring at the blank wall behind me.

Nanu is Viral-X-positive.

Nanu is Viral-X-positive! Wait, what? *WHAT?!*

My limbs felt numb as I ran out of the room towards Nanu. He must've seen me and sensed the foreboding. He stood at the doorway, looking enquiringly. He saw the look in my eyes and raised a hand to stop me from coming closer.

"WAIT! Just wait right there. What has happened? Has my report come in?"

I wasn't functioning right, and had lost all ability to form words that made sense. Rithvik stepped in and broke the news: "Nanu… I-it's positive. You're Viral-X- positive."

Nanu raised both his hands as a gesture to calm us down, "*Bass*. Okay. It's all okay."

He started inching backwards. Just before he shut the door, he called out, "You have to be strong, bete. I'm okay. Just stay safe. I'll be okay." Saying that he started receding, continuing to peep out at us till the door clicked into its frame, firmly isolating him inside.

Guilt. That was the loudest feeling tonight among all the competing ones— and there were many.

I let him spend this day alone, all by himself. He would've been worried himself, wouldn't he? Of course, he didn't complain once. His protective instincts must've taken over like they always did, and he always had to be the brave one so that I wasn't scared. He deserved better today.

Instead, I did what I have always done—prioritised things that, when it counted, just did not matter. As I retraced my day, I realised that I had made a choice. I chose *this* day to market a product that had failed before, capitalising on this fear that I was now drenched in, instead of spending the day with Nanu, even if from across the doorway, assuring him that we would make it through whatever happens as he would have for me.

Why are the most obvious things hardest to see?

WAS THIS KARMA FOR THAT TURMERIC TIP? Even my thoughts yelled within me. Sure, it wasn't the most sensitive, but when had a pinch of turmeric ever hurt anyone?

Time. That is the entire game, isn't it? If I spend the majority of my time, which basically means a majority of my day, doing things I barely like for things the world has told me I should want, where will there be any time left for the things I truly love? I was caught up inside my head again. I often find myself caught doing this math of life like there's an equation I'm missing that is meant to solve the entire puzzle. I wasn't very good at it back in school, and I'm no better now. As I try to dissect where I'm going wrong and why where I was *felt* wrong, I scrounge for references in my life for people who have, in fact, made it. Made a life that is meaningful but also enjoyable. Even and especially to the liver. Out of nowhere, my mind throws up the gleeful picture of River, about to jump, with his hands wide open, welcoming life in.

12:04 a.m.

Tell me again, why do you do what you do?

Swimming in my thoughts, I hadn't even realised when I had opened Instagram. River was online, just like our entire generation usually is, at this witching hour of midnight. Everyone except my husband, who has taken it upon himself to watch every sunrise like it's going to be different every day.

Hello to you too!

Why do you do what you do?

I needed an answer.

And what about doing it makes you feel...right?

Well

...

The three dots played for a while on my screen before his answer reached me. I stayed glued to this chat like my life depended on it.

That moment on the edge...

You can't afford the questions that don't matter there.

In that moment, you suddenly know the ones that do, the ones worth risking it all for.

It doesn't hold any answers—those come from you.

But all the questions find perspective.

Stripped down to your basic instincts, you finally meet yourself....

Stripped down... I ponder over the phrase as he continues typing. It is funny that it takes a stripping down to get to the things that matter.

Our measurements are skewed.

The edge is proof.

Certain moments are longer than others.
They occupy more space in our minds,

sometimes so much more, that it just has to expand to accommodate it.
Then, we call it growth.

Just a moment lived fully can stretch across a lifetime.

But a gazillion years spent without consciousness are as good as being non-existent.

It is the same as sleeping through time.

So how short or long your life is depends entirely on how you spend your moments.

I love how, in the English language, you say 'spend' for time—the language did not miss out this time.

It is true. It is an expense of your most valuable, arguably your only real currency.

So, cheap coins or the rarest gems?

Were your moments today long enough to be enough?

I shut my eyes, my answer unbearable. I don't answer.

We talk about life being too short, but if spent right, it really is enough.

It is just right, and it is just enough.

In making people bungy, I gift wrap that nugget of information and gift it to them in that experience.

It's something else to witness it:
When people are standing at the edge, there is a fervent energy that rises to the surface.

This is the force of life that drives it, making them realise how much existed there in the first place.

It comes from the fear of letting go and the need to cling on.

This is where gratitude is born from. Gratitude for what is.

Then rises the burning desire to dive into the unknown, the quest for thrill, the curiosity to experience something new.

This reveals the excitement there is to be found in the human experience of pursuit—to reach for something, to strive for something.

People often forget that in the stability of well-established routines and then wonder why daily living feels mundane.

And in the middle, there's faith. Faith to make that journey.

In me, to guide them and in themselves, to overcome the demons inside their own head.

When I bungy jump, I experience this allll.

To become aware of myself, my fears, my curiosity, my desire, my oneness with the world, my capabilities, and indeed, my every breath, the beating of every heartbeat—all in a matter of a moment or two, is nothing short of magic.

To give that experience to another is to empower—
That's why I do this.

That is why it feels right.

I let it sink in. I can't relate to a single one of those emotions. But what I am, in fact, starving for, I realise with a jolt, was that kind of passion. The kind of passion that makes me write essays about my joy to anyone who'd ask. I hear my body sigh. Without that passion, all of time is a purse full of clinking coins. It may look like a lot—but it isn't really.

Wow.

I have never felt that way.

I don't even know what to say.

Have I done this all wrong? I sit there, immersed in a terrible feeling of having missed the right bus. And the reroute having taken me away from Nanu and everything that could be.

Well then. I'm glad you found me.
So I can show you that life can be felt this way too, you know?

I don't mean to preach. I only have my experience to speak of.

But I do get to feel that way every day, so it must exist, right?

I mean... wow and all, but whoever feels that way, man? Who is really happy about the rigmarole of everyday living? As far as I can see, I don't find it anywhere. This weird sense of... what is it—joy? This man, by his mere ways of thought, was a bit of a challenge to my worldview. Actually, he had no 'ways'. He just felt, and he flowed from there with the audacity to be free. But there were rules to living. Had he missed the memo? Either this man was putting on a show, or he was really, really lucky.

I wonder why it's so hard to accept the *different* without finding reasons to disqualify it for. Well, it's only me who stands to lose out by dismissing as fantasy what my reality simply refuses to accommodate. I'm going to believe this. I need to do better.

Questioning the little boxes and cages I could now see tying me down, I began to type.

But.

It's like the world tells you: you should want XYZ to have a successful life.

And then, like a horse with blinders on, you start chasing those things.
The right education, an appropriate amount of travel, a good job, marriage at a decent age, a child before it's too late.
And before you know it, that's the rest of your life.
When do you get to question what YOU truly want? If you even want any of those things.

If your joy lies outside somewhere entirely different?
You spend your youth thinking of happiness as something that exists ahead, in the future,
and you keep making decisions that you think help get you there.

I was rambling now. But I was due a rant, what with everything I'm not saying these days.

In your twenties, you do everything as an investment.

Like if you follow this blueprint, you will find fulfilment tomorrow.

That anticipation of happiness—marketed as hope—keeps you excited in the moment, and you mistake it for validation that you're okay.

But before you know it,

most of your moments have passed you by,
your youth is on its way out, and you are still none the wiser.
Eventually, you get to the tomorrow where you thought this

Big golden pot of fulfilment exists, only to realise you've been totally scammed!
In your thirties, then, one has to wonder
what is tomorrow if not a sum of my todays?
So then, what about today?
But by then, your decisions have been made, and you've settled into some kind of stability that is just about taking root.

And so as not to disturb it, you just live with it,

all passion and joy slowly draining out of you, resigning to the fate of dragging your feet through the rest of your days.

I've been scammed, and I want a refund!!!!

My mind was racing furiously; my hands almost shook. I am keenly aware that I'm spiralling. If this is a late quarter-life crisis or an early onset of a midlife crisis, I don't know! Well, with all this mental health trauma coming to the fore, at least I'm digitally eligible to be woke now. Give me my halo already.

Why was I here? There was no reason to be. Born in this golden age with no dictatorship, no oppression, no slavery. I had skipped the worst of history and had started from where all my choices were my own. This generation had evolved to have sprouted metaphoric wings but seemed to have also inherited their cage: life's most basic questions seemed to have remained the same—Who am I? Why am I? How to *be*, so I can be happy? How very rudimentary, how very old, such an absolute cliché and yet so elusive.

Nanki, there are as many ways to live as there are people.

Limited stay those that can see but a few templates.
But blind are those who cannot imagine a world
beyond what they can see.
There is a Zen saying,

No snowflake ever falls in the wrong place.

I scrunched up my forehead, trying to place this within context.

Huh. What does that mean?

I was trying to grasp all that I could. It was a lot to take in for today, but it was precisely because of the kind of day it had been that I had arrived at these questions.

How you feel is valid.

Your feelings are as real as you are.

Just be careful to detangle your own feelings from those of a loud, shouting world.
How you feel is exactly how you are meant to be feeling.
Of that, I am a firm believer.
Follow the trail,
Be fierce about following it,
don't be afraid,
and then
have the courage to follow through.
Just like if you're Bungy Jumping ☺

Hmph.

How did I feel?

It was bizarre to think that I didn't know how I felt outside of the blueprint of life I had inside my head, which came from God knows where.

But you're right. It is a shouting world.

There is so much noise.

It's inside me now. Everyone else's voices.

> So much so that I can't tell my own apart anymore.
> How do I listen to what I feel?

To be three decades old and be asking strangers on the internet about how to feel—how very millennial of me.

He seemed to be typing and deleting and then typing some more. Then I finally get one long... poem?

> These words we hide behind
> are merely the cloak we've dressed our thoughts in
>
> A facade to make emotion presentable.
> They reveal but a part—the face hiding the heart:
> and therein lies its greatest sin.
>
> Because, like almost every human creation,
>
> It is so terribly limited—our flawed idea of a conversation.
>
> For it is too little and it is too small
> Compared to the dialogue of our soul,
>
> Because this energy between us
> A language of its own, above all
> —that was created by God.
> My hope for us is thus:
> Let's stay silent awhile
> and finally converse.

It's confirmed. This man is utterly jobless. Despite myself, though, I smile.

So, you're a poet too now?

The mountains make a poet out of everyone.

...

Did you find my answer here?

Did I? I read up again, and nope, I didn't really, but I have a people-pleasing thing around strangers that makes me want to reassure him.

I think I did...

You listen to yourself the same way you listen to anyone else. You simply ask first.

I find that all our answers lie in asking the right questions.

Your most important dialogue is going to be the one you have with yourself.

Make it count.

Cut out the noise and crank up your own internal volume.

And how do you do it?

Ah. I see his point now. I feel a surge of affection towards him for helping me sort through my thoughts. This time, I'm sure of the answer

I find my silence.

Et voila!

Chapter 11

There comes a point to fear, beyond which exists a unique numbness. Hovering there, was an eerie silence and a quiet alertness: a waiting in the wings for the demons to show up. I live there now. Over the next few days, I became accustomed to this perpetual discomfort. It became routine to wake up wondering if we would need a hospital bed today. Sanitising every spoon and every towel going in and out of Nanu's room became as normal as dusting the rest of the house. He was just a door away but so out of reach, we couldn't even share air. The only thing flowing freely between us was music. It floated out of his room every day, letting us know that he was getting by. Like the Azaan that rises from a mosque, it threw on a thick blanket of hope, inviting us to have faith and hold on. Of course, we video-called him, but most days, he held it awkwardly, showing barely a part of his face or sometimes a corner of his eye—both eyes, if we were lucky. His cough seemed to be getting more aggressive, though. Rithvik also suspected that he had lost his sense of taste when he didn't even care for my bread pudding that he could never help taking second servings of.

Nanu wasn't an emergency enough to get an oxygen concentrator for yet, so every now and then, if he did feel a shortness of breath while inhaling, he would just have to gulp in air, fumbling in the darkness for a single breath. This really kept us on edge. What were we supposed to hope for? That he gets sick enough to qualify for treatment? It was painful to hear him gasp. But it wasn't too often.

Today, there was Kishore Kumar on loop and *Pal Pal Dil Ke Paas* filled our house with the feeling that I identify as home. I slumped down onto my sofa around noon and allowed myself a smile. It seemed like forever since I had had a reason to. That there was no reason to grieve today, felt like a solid enough excuse for the indulgence. Rithvik was on a call with his parents, an unusual occurrence. Guys have weird relationships with their families. They are okay to speak once a month-ish and on an SOS basis. My parents, on the other hand, need an update on every meal I've eaten. A WhatsApp group exists for that very purpose. Today, mother dearest has been burning bay leaves with a prayer written on them in black sketch pen for Nanu and believes this remedy to have magical properties.

"I saw butterflies in our tea garden today. You know what that means, na?" Mum was exuberant on the video call.

I wish I didn't. I sigh into the phone, "Hmmm."

"Angels! They're around, and they're listening. Such a good sign."

I glance towards Dad standing behind her, and we share the look we always do, telepathically rolling our eyes, not visible to the naked eye, for Mum's sake. There had always been something otherworldly about her. Like she was hanging on to this realm by forced strands of gossamer. Dad was *very* much of this world but always played along, never once rationalising. He just feigned interest and let her be crazy. Now *that's* old-school romance.

"You remember Rishikesh, Ma? They have this bungy jumping there now. See, that's something we have never done."

"Bungy jumping? Why on earth would people do that? Aren't there enough ways to die? Oh, I think everyone's just bored out of their minds, honestly! Too much luxury and excess of time. Don't you be thinking about it, Nanki. I'm warning you."

I rolled my eyes, "I'm thirty-three. Please stop."

"Haan, thirty-three and thinking of jumping off a cliff. *Waah,* very grown up."

"Dad, please speak to your wife. She's out of control."

"Yes, but what to do now?" Dad shakes his head and smiles at the phone.

We spoke till we had to resume the day, and I wondered how many times River would have to deal with questions like that. I decided to add to it.

2:30 p.m.

WHY would people subject themselves to simulated fear?

It is awful in here.

River was online right now, and he got to me right away, as announced by the three dots.

To overcome it.

Aah. Well played.

So you're saying

it's not so much about fear as it is about courage, isn't it?

That's why people must throw themselves off the bridge in Bungy.

Well, yes, and no.

Of course, the victory at the end of the battle is phenomenal.

You can feel that rejoicing trickle down to your soul.

And trust me, it IS mental warfare at the edge.

But the part before, the meeting with your own fears, IS its own experience.

I've Bungy jumped for the majority of the last three decades and got tens of thousands to experience it for themselves.

Yet, it is like nothing I can put into words.

It holds the power to drown you out or to propel you into a flight. The choice is yours.

Mental warfare? Yep, definitely sounds about right. That simulated fear, as well as this that I was drowning in.

But it's terrible to have to face fears.

It's worse to live with them.

Mic drop moment. Due silence given.

Then, after a minute—

How do people get the courage to overcome it?

It's not so much a 'get' as it is a gathering of courage. Until you need it, you don't know it exists within you.

Another reminder of our own infinity, isn't it?

Sometimes, we are beyond our own reach.

It is just that under stress, we have to catch up.

The choice is this:
Which part of yourself do you feed:
The fear of the fall or the chance to fly?
This choice becomes a mood, and a mood can become your whole personality.
It spills into daily living, too: do you shrink down into the safe and familiar?
Or do you dare to go beyond and rise into the unknown?

Shrink down into the safe and familiar or dare to go beyond. The words hit a chord. I just thought of something.

You know, I just realised.

I might be a thousand kilometres away from your bridge.

Yet, I am already at the edge too.

So help me understand it.

Because I need to figure out what my choice is and how to follow through when I do.

All I can tell with certainty is that it too feels like standing on the brink of war.

And you're right about it feeling like mental warfare. It is.

I figured if you could manage to take me to Rishikesh, you could help me walk down this bridge till I get to the edge too.

You see, there are a ton of questions and much fewer answers.

Since you sell courage for a living, can you help me gather mine?

From wherever it exists inside me.

If it does, that is.

At this point, I frankly don't know.

He must think I'm crazy. Somehow, I don't care what he thinks of me—why would I? I barely know him. Not in real life, anyway. Weirdly enough, that helped. I wonder why it is easier to be honest with strangers about internal battles.

I look at Rithvik. He's on his laptop, tired from the day already, and it's not even lunchtime yet. Maybe it's because everyone I know was in equal suffrage. Or in different kinds of suffering, but rather equally. How could someone bleeding themselves bandage the wounds of another anyway? Not to mention how selfish it would be to dump my grievances on my own people. I was as empty in helping them as I knew they would be to me.

Not that River may not have issues of his own, nor that he may not be dealing with this breakdown of the world himself; well, he did seem to be dealing with it better. Besides, I did not know of them, and maybe that's why I can pretend that those burdens were not mine to carry. Also, maybe because from this distance, I could imagine him to be just perfect, in perpetual peace and harmony, having all the answers to every question figured out.

He was the unknown factor, oddly sitting in the middle of a puzzling equation. My puzzling equation. Assuming a value—any value—to x only helped get closer to the solution. Even if, in the end, x=0.

It was a whole minute before he finally said something.

It's what I am here for :)

It's settled, then! I bring you my fears and you teach me of courage.

I smiled. In a weird way, I felt somewhat secure in knowing that someone out there had my back. Or, in this case, the metaphoric rubber chords. I chuckled at that thought.

Deal.

First things first. I had to open this conversation. If I was serious about my chat with River, which I intended to be, I had to start somewhere, and it had to be here. As uncomfortable as it makes me, I do have to invite in those I was walking this journey with.

"Rithvik." I blinked hard. I wasn't sure what made me so nervous.

I had gone over this conversation over and over in my head last night, and yet it wasn't fully thought through. There was this weird energy building up, but I hadn't quite figured out the why, how, and where of it all. I knew that I did, but I had to get it out already, even though I knew that in none of those hypothetical conversations did I sound sane or convincing, even to myself.

Rithvik looked up from his laptop, his stubble glistening with a few greys. He was awfully quiet these days, buried under a pile of work, keeping to himself. The more that we were in each other's face, the less we seemed to know what went on behind it.

"You know, I was thinking. I don't... see the p-point of my work anymore," I blurted in a rush.

He blinked twice as hard, "Errr, money?"

"I'm not enjoying it."

"Tch!" He shrugged in agreement like it was the most normal tragedy in the world. "I'm sorry, Nan." He turned back to his laptop.

"I mean it!" I said, pushing through.

He looked up again, widening his eyes now.

"Okayy? No one is, not right now." He was looking at me keenly, wondering why I was stating the obvious all of a sudden.

"No, but I mean. It isn't making sense to me anymore," I was dangerously close to breaking down. Again, I wasn't sure why.

"How can we... I waste... it's futile, all of it. Of all my choices and my entire life."

He frowned, surprised.

"Including me?" he says it slowly, and there's clearly more where that came from, but right now is not about him, and his clinginess will have to wait.

"What? Of course not. I'm talking about advertising, or maybe just this job. Or maybe just this project... I don't know."

Should've figured that out before I started down this road.

He holds my gaze, his expression unreadable. For what feels like five minutes, he says nothing, and I don't look away.

See, this is why I don't process with people. Even with the best intentions, they never know how to handle you when you know you need... handling. He keeps tugging for more of me, and now, when I'm giving it to him, he's doing exactly what I always suspected him to do: rejecting me. See? I was right. Our dynamic works as long as I stay self-sufficient and give him the bits of warmth he asks for. The moment I actually bring to the table something I care about or my needs, poof! The balance of power changes, the chaser becomes the master, and I'm out in the cold, all by myself once again.

"You're just feeling guilty you couldn't be there for Nanu that day and the days before his isolation because you were occupied by your meetings." Rithvik's tone is flat and emotionless.

He wasn't wrong.

"So what if I am?" my voice was rising without permission. I feel frustrated that he refuses to understand the gravity of how I feel.

He looks at me like I'm crazy. "So calm down."

Urgh, the argument kryptonite. No 'calm down' in the history of calming people down has ever calmed anyone down.

"I don't feel calm! I don't feel okay. That's the point!"

His face twisted, trying to understand what trip I was on, "So what do you want?" He sounded flabbergasted now.

"I don't know!" I'm affronted by his tone. I guess trying to think things aloud with your partner is too much to ask for. He sighs deeply and resets his face to a kinder expression.

"Nanki, isn't there too much upheaval already?"

Honestly, he just sounded tired. I couldn't even blame him. This whole thing had been exhausting. From the outside, it may look like a lack of movement meant an extended holiday of sorts, but the mental fatigue was real. Amidst everything else, there were still EMIs* to pay, salaries to be given, food and medical supplies to be bought, and enough savings to be able to afford treatment just in case. If they would be so lucky to even get it, that is. It didn't help that the 'just in case' could be any bizarre amount of money. There really was no telling.

I silence my thoughts.

He was right. What was I thinking?

For a moment, I had dared to hope. For what, I wasn't quite sure; just for something… bigger. He must've sensed my energy deflate because his voice had softened considerably when he said, "Nanki, there is too much happening to be thinking clearly. Let's not uproot any more things right now, okay? Quite frankly, I have no bandwidth to deal with any more changes. Do you?"

I stay silent, not breaking eye contact.

He continues, "I mean, is this great? No, of course not. I wish I could take a break. I wish I could somehow make money making frothy coffees or actually just play cricket. I'm hanging on by the edge of my teeth to this job because I want to see this company through and because what other options do I really have?

"We're doing it for this: We are working on half our salaries, and you know if things don't change soon, we'd still have to dip into our savings within two months. Just to maintain the life we have now. What about next year? We are supposed to be having children at some point… How are we supposed to do this without holding on to whatever little stability we do have?"

Dammit. If he's going to go all rational on me… how would ridiculous dreams ever get fed? I frown. This was check and mate, and just like that, I was trapped into the smallest square space of life. The problem with asserting equality was the acceptance that it went both ways. Just like I couldn't imagine Rithvik leaving his job to 'rethink' his life, jeopardising our comfort and stability, it wasn't fair of me to leave all our combined financial burdens on him either.

'Hmm . . . ' I nod resignedly. He gives me a weak smile. This is what it was going to be. This is all my life was going to be.

He walks over to me to give me a hug, and I shrug him off. Just because he's right doesn't mean I'm not upset. He grins and settles for pulling my cheek instead, tucking a strand of hair behind my ear. Here's the thing, though: when you start understanding the gravity of death, you learn to weigh life—the thought gurgled up—demanding to be heard. When it was so damn hard to stay alive, shouldn't living amount to more, somehow? Otherwise, what was the point of putting up such a fight? These thoughts sprung up from somewhere deep inside my core but froze into a lump in my throat as I turned away, stifling the tears welling up in my eyes.

Chapter 12

WHAT, woman? WHAT do you need to say?

Some weird, unprompted restlessness swirled through my body, and my mind seemed to be mumbling something ineligible. I'm trying to listen in, but I can't seem to.

'The mountains make a poet out of everyone', I remember River saying. Taking his cue, I feel the bizarre need to find the poetry within me so as to lend these scattered emotions some much-needed words. Maybe then, they would stand a chance to exist. I scroll up till I find the first image River had ever sent me. The stoic mountain ranges, bejewelling Rishikesh late at night. Unchanging and majestic. I remember the tranquillity I felt that night and borrow from it now. It was harder to come by now. What was it about something that had existed since far before us—and will continue to, long after us that makes it such a source of calm? Maybe it's the standing testimony that some things are capable of weathering far more than we would ever have to. The mountain ranges witnessing an eternity and us, a mere ephemeral moment in the landscape of time. And yet they survive. So maybe, just maybe, I stand a chance too.

All the struggles in the world were to become bigger, and yet, ironically, comfort was only found in feeling terribly small. I started to write.

4:45 p.m.

What an odd moment in time,
To be feeling
The weight and the weightlessness,
The meaning,
And the meaninglessness,
The purpose and the purposelessness
of the Artist and his Art,
Of Strife and its striving
Of Life and its living.

It felt important somehow to document this point in life to remember where it got me. There was nothing remarkable about it. Really. But it needed to be flagged. I left it on River's DMs. I don't know why. Maybe because it's somewhere I can be seen, without being seen I guess as casually as leaving a note in my personal diary. I'd reflect upon it later. This window was becoming my personal diary where I wondered all my random wonderments, but even better because it responded back. Who knew River would end up becoming this to me when I responded to that Bungy advertisement an aeon ago? He wasn't online, and that's fine. To talk is great, but to be unconditionally heard is infinitely better. I give a dry smile and leave the chat to proceed with the rest of my day.

8:00 p.m.

Is everything okay on your end?

River had hearted the poem. I realise that while I've spoken of life and living as a concept, I hadn't once discussed my real every day. That's how most conversations happen on the app, but it did feel odd to feel like you almost know someone without knowing a thing about them. It was time to change that.

It's my grandfather. He is Viral-X-positive.

Silence. Then, a minute later:

Oh, I am sorry to hear that.

Are you tiding through?

Now, *that* felt like a real question I could answer. An empty show of solidarity only avoids having to dig deep enough to engage with the awkwardness of unstable emotions. I remembered having placated Kavya with empty words, and it had NOT been okay. I feel grateful for the chance to have my struggle acknowledged. I take it.

Actually, I am not.

I am struggling.

Tremendously.

With fear, with uncertainty, with making sense of any of this.
With understanding what it means to be alive in a dying world,
with the guilt of it, The unshakeable, unbearable guilt.
Of not doing better with that privilege.
Of having such a living not amount to anything.

A living that is as good as not.

I type the words furiously, mad at the world for throwing such a tantrum.

Yep. I read the message before sending it. That about begins to cover it.

So we're not talking about Viral-X anymore, are we?

I guess we're not.

WHY are you this unhappy?

That's how I come across, don't I? Like a brat. I don't care. Which is, *ahem,* also the brat slogan, I guess. But this question was almost ... *cute.*

Only psychopaths must be happy all the time!

Hahahah now that's the wisest thing you've ever said.

Yes, no one can be happy all the time. It is true.

It is nothing to aspire for because it can never be real.
The human condition is far more complex than that.

I think about that now. I never did earlier because I didn't have the time to think about things like happiness before lockdown. Now that I do, I see it all ever so clearly.

Yes...Happiness has had quite the rebrand.

It's being aggressively sold...like cornflakes was at one point.
As an essential.

As a thing that you're wrong not to have.
As something you're flawed without.

Of course, everyone wants to be happy,
but to make the conversation this flat and one-dimensional
is just warped.

I mean, people have always craved happiness, but the kind of obsession people have right now is truly mental. Like any obsession, it's washing out the other colours of the spectrum entirely. You don't even realise when you've become a victim to it.

Exactly!

We have to experience a myriad of emotions.
I say 'have to' because we do. No one is exempt from it.

We have to feel everything there is to feel.

That is the nature of being alive.

But then we have to strive to create contentment amidst that chaos.
That is the nature of being human.

So, a more valid question to ask would be: Are you unhappy then?
Because if it is so, you will have to listen to your unhappiness.

Restlessness will persist for as long as you don't.
That is the nature of restlessness, no?

I think about that. I take a minute to think about it, in fact. Then five.

I guess I must be. Happy, I mean.
In the sense that I am not sad.

And yet ...

I wondered if I should go on and decide upon it.

Something is missing.

Something has been missing for a while.

What makes joy so tedious in a perfectly good life?

It's like... There is a little seed of void that sprouts up out of nowhere on some of the most ordinary days.

I don't know how to explain it...

After careful consideration, typing, and erasing, and then typing some more, I finally write:

It feels like a moist spot on freshly dried sheets.

I sit back and revel in this response. It's a masterpiece because I can't imagine anything else do a better job of explaining it.

I once tried placing its physical location in my body.

When I pictured it inside me, it looked like a little black hole in the centre of my chest that sucked the joy out of my heart and limbs

and spat it into the infinity of the universe, where it would be lost forever.

Do you know what's weird?
In those moments, I almost wished that something really was wrong,

so I could give it a reason.

I never found one, so maybe it was me.
Before I could fix that, though, the humdrum of the day would drown the thought out and lull me into an unthinking living I was more familiar with.

And the moment would pass just like it came.

I guess
it's easy to forget the noise of your thoughts
when you're too busy going through the paces of a well-planned life,
designed to be the best version of average.

The great Indian dream.

Till the world fell apart.
If I was finding reasons to blame, I had no excuses now.
What a yay, right?
Nowhere to hide from them anymore, and no exit left open.

I had to sit with it, didn't I?

The more I thought about it, the more aggressively it grew,
As if the more attention I gave it, the more I kept feeding it.

It wasn't just a little black hole anymore,
it became this big, growing darkness threatening to consume me.

Some days, I think...it is now feeding on me instead.

The bigger it becomes, the smaller I become,
Till the blackness is everywhere and the light is just a speck.
If at all.

He took a while to respond, and I don't blame him.

Nanki, I have a question.

Where are you?

Where inside your body do you think you are?

Are you your skin, your eyes, your heart?

I looked down at myself. I looked at my hands and turned my palms up. *Nope.* I looked at my legs and twitched my toes. *Nope.* That stubby toe can't exactly be where I'm dwelling. Prettified as it was with the glittery nail polish: testimony to the things one does when they aren't bound by the protocols of playing an adult. I touch my palm to my chest, trying to feel my heartbeat. It was mine, and yet I don't know how my heart feels to the touch or about the life it was leading inside of me. I wonder if it feels cared for, even though I had never really looked after it, not consciously, anyway. I pretty much expected it to do that for itself. And it did, I guess. I mean, I don't smoke ... does that count? Oh, wait, that's for the lungs. Um, I'm sure the heart is hearting from it too. God, I need to stop talking like Gen-Z. It makes me sound like a boomer.

I walk up to my dresser and stand in front of the mirror. I lean in closer to look at my eyes. They seem to give away a lot. I blink deliberately, my eyes continuing to stare at themselves. Was I my eyes? They feel more like the narrator. Not the story. *Nope.* My body, my organs, and the blood running through them all feel like the caretakers outside of me—protecting me, holding me. They were all an intrinsic part of my being but not the being itself. Then, where am I? What are they taking care *of*? I could feel my breath move up and down inside me. My aliveness seemed to be intertwined with it.

Am I my breath?

I sputter the words out loud even as I write them, exasperated.

A breath is such a fascinating thing.

You take in air that already exists outside, consume it till it fills you up, and release it in the next second, leaving a void for another.

Essentially, you draw from infinity and let it flow through you briefly, leaving you and itself changed by its mere passage through you.

Isn't that so cool?

You consume a bit of infinity, and it consumes a bit of you

and then, you release it back unto itself,
although now, with a bit of you
until one day, you finally become one with it entirely.

I am suddenly extremely conscious of every breath, and it seems to hasten under the glare of this microscope.

Erm River.

Are you saying I don't exist at all?

You know, how kids feel watching a magic trick being pulled off? That's how I feel. Spooked is the word you're looking for, where I've somehow been magicked out of my own damn self. Seriously though, physically speaking, where the hell AM I?

On the contrary, ma chérie,

You exist infinitely.
You are not your body.

You are nowhere in your body, and you are everywhere, all at once.

The question is WHAT am I?

The concept of 'I' must then be beyond the body. The body is simply our vessel.

I think about Nanu and his breath. I wonder if the infinity was planning on reclaiming his piece of itself, leaving his body behind. Do I dare to ask, knowing fully well that nothing might suffice?

Then why do we fear death so much?

We have always been afraid of what is bigger than us, haven't we? Infinity always scares us. Terrifies us, in fact.

One always loves the waves but forever fears the ocean.

I think what is frightening is the inherent knowledge that you cannot contain it but rather, that you are contained by it.

Isn't that rather arrogant?

To not embrace it just because we do not understand it.

And yet, we do it all the time.

In life, as well as on the subject of death.

We can meet them both with equal equanimity.

Sometimes, I wonder if he's smoking some magic mushrooms or something. He very well could be; whoever knows? I wouldn't mind getting in on that action. Only sometimes, though, when I really needed answers.

One *garma garam chai,* on the other hand, worked just fine for when the questions got too much.

I find the shaking-my-head emoji and send it.

Equity, I understand. Equanimity, whaaa?

I did google for the word again because it is not an easy one.

It is integral to my experience, so I know it and know of it.

It is the mastery of the mind to stay calm amidst chaos.

Not in a submissive way but rather in a very carefully controlled manner.

I don't have this item.

I say it flatly because I truly don't.

Sure, you do.

I can prove it to you.

You know how when you enter a room, you can sense the tension before you've heard a single word?

When you hear of betrayal, how do you instantly have that sense of dawning,

like you knew this was coming, even before your mind has accepted it?

When you hear of someone you love dying, despite frantically going into denial, there is a part inside of you that goes cold and just knows this has happened.

On the flip side, before a winning pitch, how do you know you've got this?

How do you feel the love of those who are far away?

There is a place within you of inherent knowledge that is wise beyond your years and senses—what we like to call our gut feeling.

Took me a while, but I know to trust it now.

My profession helped—it made me hypersensitive to the rise and fall of my energy and emotions.

When they oscillate in intense extremes, you realise very quickly that only the one who is not troubled by the waves can ride the tide.

I guess that's why assertive peace became a natural coping mechanism and a subject of intrigue for me.

Something I've since spent a long time studying.

That's why he was so good at this, obviously. This hippie, magic-mushroom-y language that, on the wrong day, I guarantee I would've dismissed as wishy-washy nonsense. That's not today. It comes naturally to him—this assertive peace.

How do I get this in the here and now?

That would be for you to figure out.

All I know is there is strength in knowing that the soul is eternal.

Haven't you heard, we were born from the stars in the beginning of time?

We carry them within us.

And so never has there been a time where your spirit has not existed, nor will there ever be one where you cease to be.

What isn't will never be. What is, will never cease to be.

So, where is there any need for fear?
What is there left to do but just be alive?
Fully, wholly,
Really.

Fully, wholly... really, I repeated in a whisper to the empty room.

I had goosebumps crawl up on my skin. It was electrifying, this thought, but it was also pacifying. How extremely odd. River went on, freeing me from the need to respond. He was teaching me—no, it was less patronising than that. He was sharing *his* experience of living with me and allowing me to make it my own. The oldest iCloud in the world: Empathy. Put your feelings out there, and it exists for as long as its memory does, to be drawn from, to be inspired by, to build upon. If only one cares to open the album.

You know what I see when I see people combat their fears?

That this duel with the dark exists in every moment.
Some moments, we just sleep through it; others force us to wake up to it.

Some moments, it sneaks in and drowns us under,

In others, it honourably stands in front of us, forcing us to fight.

Like a moment at the edge—and isn't that so much better?
This duel between the light and the dark will always continue
till one consumes the other,
just like the day consumes the night,
and the night plunders the day,
going around in circles in an unending loop.

Oh, but when there is light...

Oh yes, indeed. I walk into my balcony to see the streetlamps coming on. It was too late for tea and too early for dinner. There's nothing to do but watch those lights flicker. Not the worst bargain.

Why is it then, that the first thing that the dawn of light does
is cast shadows,
pulling along a piece of darkness?

As if teasing it out to challenge itself?

That is a good question.

I would think that that's the law of the land.

Look at the creation of existence:

You have been given a life, and no matter how you live it, it is going to culminate in its death.

You have been given a functioning body, but it must always be in need of fuel through water and food.

You have been given a mind that will always have to cope with restlessness

You have been given energy,
but you will have to overcome inertia.

You have been given wisdom,
but you must spend a lifetime unlearning first.

You have been given a whole life,
but you have to make it through every day.

Tell me about it.

When you put it like that, I want to hug every human and apologise.

Sounds like God is a masochist, and we are the sufferers. What an inefficient system. Perpetually in need to just basically survive.

How awful is that!

Oh, but don't you see?
How beautiful that is....
We weren't just given an existence; we were also given its purpose.

Pretty neat, in fact, isn't it?
We are alive, we have desires,
we therefore strive, and in that striving,
we create our living'

I paced within the little space and considered that. Something about this ... doesn't sound right, wisdom-wise.

Definitely relatable and all, but wasn't evolution supposed to be about going beyond the pettiness of this animalistic 'real' living?

Aren't we supposed to move towards giving up all worldly desires though?

Isn't that the ultimate benchmark of growth? To find peace in forsaking desires and material gains and earthly attachments?

Detachment and moksha and all that jazz.

Maybe it's different in France, I wonder.

You're confusing inherent desires with impulses.

One of the lamps refused to come on and stayed unlit. I feel a sudden hatred for it.

How can you tell the difference?

By how it feels, of course.

Our feelings are our greatest internal compass—our one guiding light.

If we can figure out how to tune into it, it will lead us to the shore.

Impulses will feel like passionless play.

Scattered pursuits, the more of which you have, the more of it you will need.

Inherent desires are different: those will feel like prayer.

The deeper you dive into them, the lesser you will be wanting for.

It feels like the truth emerging and taking you along into its glorious wave.

The more you pursue it, the fuller you will get.

...Aah, now I get why it must be called fulfilment.

I trace the word in my mind along with him and observe how much more beauty can be seen when standing on the outside. I think this is the first time I think of standing on the outside as a beautiful thing.

Yes, it must, mustn't it?

Thanks, River. I should be getting back now.

Oh, and by the way, how is your English so good?

Thank you for thinking that!
I had to be able to communicate with my jumpers when they were scared for their life!
Learning their language is the only way I can show up.

I also know a little Hindi, but it's limited to the cook at my local Dhaba when I need to tell him the food is *'bohot acha hai'.*

I grin, imagining his accented Hindi, then look into the living room and sigh; dinner wouldn't cook itself.

Bohot acha hai.

I leave the chat inspired. I think I'm going to make *Dhaba Aloo* today.

Chapter 13

It is another evening, and I brush through my hair, looking into the mirror. Rithvik is buried in his laptop on the couch outside. He's gone back to behaving like it wasn't a big deal at all, and that's slightly maddening. It's the dismissal of the subject, the indifference, that makes it final and unbearable. I honestly worry that one of these days, he's going to feel like he's made a big mistake with me because I'm clearly too much for him to handle anyway. He always seemed the tiniest bit besotted with what he couldn't figure out, and six years back, that was me. It's entirely possible that he was in it for the supposed mystery, and if he's realising that where he expected intrigue, there's just… chaos, he isn't showing it.

I straighten myself and look closely at my reflection. *Me*. Not me. It really was mind-bending every time I did this. River's chat had kept coming back to me, and there was one part I wasn't sure of yet. I scrolled back.

5.15 p.m.

So, the difference between inherent desires and impulses is like the difference between being full AND/or satiated?

Those two things are not the same thing.

He was online but didn't respond for another fifteen minutes. I wonder if there were others like me that he was attending to. Putting out fires everywhere, this River.

If you say so!

😬

Hmph

But seriously, it's only worth it when you're consumed with it.

100 or nothing.

To build something solid out of your desire demands a one-pointedness.

Not an unfettered meandering, but rather consistently choosing to walk in the light of your own truth. Until all else is blinded out.

That's when you see it emerge.

And yes, that pursuit takes all the courage in the world.

Courage. The one thing I could feel depleting out of me, day after day. River must've guessed it because, after a moment, he wrote:

You think courage is about fighting what is standing opposite you when courage is, in fact, what you have to fight inside of you. Always.

Protecting the ideal by acceptance of the battle is far greater than sitting back in renunciation.

The world doesn't stop burning just because you close your eyes.

Renunciation is born from great sorrow.

By definition, it is separating oneself from the experience of living.
Sometimes, in exaggerated cases, even physically, but not always.

More often, people give up mentally and then call it wisdom. To get so jaded that you don't allow life to draw you in is always a defeat, never a victory.

It is a pulling of oneself away, tearing something apart, taking great pain to hack away at the glue that holds you together.

Renunciation, as peaceful as it sounds, is intrinsically built of grave conflict, and has anything beautiful ever come out of conflict?

Is there really strength in detachment?

At this edge in your life, you say you are at, if you were, in fact, standing at the literal edge, looking out at the vastness that is yours to conquer, in Bungy, is there strength in letting go of the desire to jump, or is there glory in letting go of your internal fears?

Perspective is a gift that you find lying behind you when you take that one step ahead.

So much of wisdom is shedding the delusions of intelligence.

It is the calm that transcends grief and anxiety.
Those exist within it, where it tears.

Peace isn't something that resides outside of you that warrants you overcoming yourself in its pursuit. It is something that comes when you align with yourself.

As an integral piece of art in the design of the universe.

That black spot you had said—sounds like it may be a tear in the being, the part where you get separated from yourself.

A sign of disconnect. Get to it so you can stitch it up.
☺

I sink into my chair. A *disconnect* from the self, a tear in the fabric of my being.

Are you suggesting I'm depressed?

I can't possibly know that.

What I do know is that when you're unwell, you lose your will to eat.

Appetite is a sign of health.

Whether it is your hunger for food or for dreams.

Attaching shame to it, then, is grossly misguided.

Sometimes, it is so much harder to know what your dreams even are. It was easier to identify the nightmares. Maybe that's where to begin—knowing what you *don't* want.

What if the chase of dreams disrupts the reality you have so carefully built?

The problem with the jump is that it takes you away from the safety of the ground.

How is that not sacrilege?

There's suddenly some commotion outside. I can hear Rithvik in the hallway. I leave my phone aside and get up to see. Rithvik was glued to Nanu's room, singing rather badly, through the door to one of Nanu's favourite songs. Nanu, in turn, cranked up the volume and started singing too. I can actually hear his raspy voice in heartwarming pieces. Out of nowhere, all of a sudden, the music had pushed its way in.

It sat oddly, wedging itself in the middle of the now permanent, although intangible, residents of the house: Emptiness and Fear. This cacophony filled our home, becoming its own entity, and took up real space, growing louder and bigger. So much so that the other two seemed to have been outweighed, forced to shrivel up, even if only briefly.

Leaning against the door frame, soaking the view in, I ask myself again: Am I happy? I look over at Rithvik, seeing the man I had married peek outside his skin after a long, long time.

I did love how loving Rithvik was to my family. Always had. I loved him for how much Nanu loved him. I loved him for how the house lit up with our togetherness. I loved how we managed to stitch together our own little world amidst the Kishore Kumar music floating in from Nanu's Caravan, me narrating my day to the last detail, and Rithvik's laughter filling up the room—and for how, in this home there was love.

That must be the same as being in love. And it must mean that there was happiness. It had always been enough. Well, some days anyway. On days like this. And days like this carried me through the others...

I run in to my phone to capture it on video. Adding it to my Instagram stories, I caption it with #CrazyStupidLove.

Before I knew it, the song had carried me into its music, and at some point, I had joined in, breaking into a dance for as long as the song lasted. Then, the day returned to normal, but it mercifully left us with a bounce to our steps and a lightness in our hearts. That's how we knew that although the song had ended, the music lived on... By the time I returned, my Instagram had a couple of unread DMs:

Sacrilege. noun.

A violation or misuse of what is regarded as sacred. Had to look it up. What a pretty word for something so devastating.

But I guess most devastating things are seen as terribly beautiful, aren't they?

We are so good at attaching such beauty to tragedy and so much virtue to suffering.

Just as I was getting lost in the poetry of his thought, he added,

Pardon my language, but THAT is utter bullshit.

I snorted.

Hahahhahahahahah, I did NOT see that coming.

It is true! The world needs to stop with it already.

Romanticising the idea of hurt and pain as a concept needs to be retired.

Your dreams and desires, your interpretation of the world and how you react to it, how life happens to you and how you happen to it, are all your unique footprints on this moment in time.

Denying any of it for a false sense of virtue, for following someone else's idea of the ideal life, now THAT is sacrilege.

It can only ever cause resentment, and you can't be of any use to anyone when all you are is a ball of resentment.

It will always get you, one day or another:
The truth that flows within you.

What a waste it would be for anyone to spend their lives diminishing themselves, becoming smaller and smaller till nothing exists anymore, just to fit into boxes that were always too small to contain them in the first place,

instead of honing those beautiful rough edges that stick out and force the box to expand instead?

I look at Rithvik. He sat across from me, humming the tune of the song we had danced to earlier, and I felt a rush of affection.

The lyrics begin playing inside my head of their own accord.

Haal kaisa hai janaab ka…

Rithvik, my anchor in a crazy world, keeping me afloat, keeping me sane by standing next to me, rock-solid—being the one constant in an increasingly maddeningly unstable world. I could never, ever hurt him. Annoying as he was sometimes.

That would be sacrilege.

Kya khayaal hai aap ka…

He looks up and, seeing me look at him, starts singing aloud now.

Hum tum to machal gaye ho ho ho…

His left shoulder joins the party in his head, doing a little dance.

Yun hi fisal gaye haa haa haaaa…'

I just sat there looking at him. This was the problem, and herein lay my conflict. I think I have, after all, turned into the oldest trope in the book: a woman very much in love and in agony and in grief, all at once—with this man, with this world, with this life.

Sometimes the stakes are too high. Sometimes you just can't.

It is a struggle that has existed since the beginning of time:

One trying so desperately to catch the voices of others in the room often turns deaf to their own.

The inability to detangle the threads, the black from the white, always plunged the world into an infinite grey.

There is a time for everything.

You won't till you can. But after that…

Eventually, we all become our own person.

When that happens, I hope you travel lighter,
And don't carry any guilt of what you leave behind or of the stakes it cost you.

And I hope that then, you remember...

That a bird's song is just as sweet even when no one hears it.

What a shame it would be if the bird wouldn't sing in the absence of an audience.

The world would lose out on the song and, far more grievously, the bird on its singing.

For the sake of its beauty, I hope we let there be song 🐦

Someday, I wish I do in fact, gather the courage to sing out my song, but today, and right now, it was time to come back home.

Chapter 14

December 23.

It was a weird thing. Of course, it had been a coincidence for me to rebrand the drink on the same day that Nanu had tested positive for Viral-X. Of course, it was. But somehow, it had gotten linked in my brain, as if one was the function of the other.

For the past ten days, I had stayed away from work after having sent a cursory mail to Jaya informing her of the crisis on the home front and of my unavailability until further notice. I wrote of Nanu having tested positive, of us having to get tested, and of our house being flagged as a containment zone. After that, I switched off without waiting for a response. I didn't exactly have the energy to open emails, check my messages, or take calls.

Whatever short-lived mojo I had gotten back seemed to have evaporated out of me like smoke as quickly as it came. I would probably never say this out loud, but I secretly hope that Nanu gets better by putting a solid distance between me and this project. Feels cursed, and even if it was just a crazy idea in my mind, I'm not willing to take a chance. If nothing else, what if these ideas become self-fulfilling prophecies? Like if you believe something hard enough, it becomes your truth?

Like *God*, I think wryly.

That's something that I have been wondering about a lot recently. With all this time I now had, with nowhere to go, with nothing in my control, I wondered about the existence of a God. I don't exactly identify as an atheist, but neither do I associate with any kind of faith. Nanu was a religious man, and I always saw mum bow her head to his God. But only in front of him, when she was here. I'm pretty sure it was more out of love for her father than for God, but she followed suit anyway without questioning it. We never discussed religion at home. Whoever believed in whatever just spoke of it as fact, no different from gravity. So, in a way, we were a bunch of people living different realities, and it was perfectly normal for them to all coexist simultaneously. Nanu would often read from his religious texts and narrate the most elaborate stories from what he referred to as sacred ancient history. Sounded like the script of a South Indian blockbuster to me, to be honest, with far more characters and *wowza* moments than I could keep track of. Then again, his reality. Mum had her *woo woo* too. Dad, well, he had himself.

In the current dire situation, however, I needed to find an object to attach my faith to. Something that could give me strength. It would make life so much easier to just believe that help was on its way. Maybe it was, maybe it wasn't. But my faith would get me through, and maybe that was helpful enough. Maybe that was what faith was about.

Since it was just an esoteric concept, it couldn't be proven. But it also couldn't be *disproven*. The more intangible, the better, because how do you destroy something that exists as a belief inside your head?

What a sneaky little caveat, marketing-wise. This concept emerges from the depths of your fears, takes the form of your highest imagination of courage, and, in doing so, gives you it. All coming from within you, all already existing within your energy field. You create the demand. You provide the supply. Your faith guarantees the transaction. That's check and mate. Truly, the greatest brand of all. *God. A self-fulfilling prophecy.*

Maybe if I believed in a divine power as hard as I believed in my fears, that would become true too, and by believing it to be so, I could intensify the protection around us all. This made practical sense. Maybe I'm woo woo too. I just find a logic to justify it. Wow, the apple truly doesn't fall far from the tree. However, the fact of the matter was that I didn't know where to start or how to really pray to please this almighty power to harness it. Anyway, my current weird superstition seems to be working because it was almost ten days, and Nanu seemed to be getting better. I would not so much as open my laptop till we could open his door.

The doctor had said that by the eleventh day, regardless of his symptoms and condition, he would no longer be contagious, and he could resume accessing the rest of the house. I was counting down the hours now. In some corner of the house, so was Rithvik.

It was nearing midnight. The tenth day was coming to a close. I was standing in my kitchen, impatiently brewing three cups of tea in anticipation, finally to be enjoyed together, huddled around him on his creaky old bed, in the same space, breathing in the same air.

I add all the spices he likes in his teas; although usually used individually, today I threw them in together: Cardamom, grated ginger, and some precious golden-orange strands of saffron. It was just about starting to smell like a festival in here, even as my phone beeped:

I read the time on my screen:

00:00

I swipe open the lock screen and jump into my WhatsApp:

It was Nanu: "I free! If awake. Hug me."

He always had trouble locating the apostrophe on the keypad.

The screen blurred in front of me as all the tension of everything seemed to wash away all at once. It was finally over. All the tears I had never cried sprung up now as I ran to his room, clutching my phone hard. He was sitting up in his bed against the headboard, freshly bathed and all dressed in his off-white kurta, the last few strands of his grey hair combed neatly back, arms open, waiting for an embrace. It was as if he had been carefully, painstakingly even, getting ready for a celebration. It *was* one. In that little room on a random midnight, huddled together in the heartiest of hugs, it was quite simply the greatest celebration there ever was. I cried, he cried, and at some point,

Rithvik had joined the hug, and amidst a flurry of kisses and tears, there was the smell of an all-spiced tea that filled the room. Rithvik had brought in a tray of my tea in our finest china and kept it on the mantle. I didn't know it then, but I would remember that fragrance for the rest of my life as the smell of a miracle.

Over the next few hours, I allowed the relief to wash over me. I, in fact, let myself get drenched in it. It was almost morning now, but the sun showed no signs of letting the world know. I wanted to scream from the rooftops and let everyone know that all was well in 26 Geetanjali Enclave. I wanted to tell the neighbours and the strangers, but first I wanted to tell Jaya. I didn't want to discuss work still. However, I feel the kind of joy right now that makes one feel ... invincible.

If I have this, I can face the rest of the world, I think, as I see Nanu snore next to me.

We had both slept the night in here. Rithvik dragged out our musty spare mattress from the storage under our bed. It was placed perpendicular to Nanu's bed, although on the floor, and he now lay on it, fast asleep. We had stayed up for another hour just talking. Of health and sickness, of fear, of courage. Also of food, of chai, and of neighbours. It was everything and nothing, really. As I lay there now, ruminating over it, I realise what a privilege it is to feel joy in the nothingness of our every day.

Funny, how that was, in fact, everything.

It's that nothingness that takes up most of the time anyway. The time in between everything, in that sneaky space that exists between things. The sliver of time between meetings and meals and social media ... when there's a peace of mind within that, it buoys up the rest, like a steady sea holding up the ship. However, when there's chaos raging within the nothingness, there's not a thing to be done to keep one from drowning. Now that I'm here in this place of peace, I picked up my phone to call Jaya. It was seven in the morning.

It rings thrice before she picks up, "It's a very good morning indeed!"

"H-Hello?" I croaked. We have switched to an upbeat setting, but my throat doesn't seem to have received the memo.

"Hallelujah, she's alive!" Jaya exclaimed, her cheery self in all its glory, way too before coffee. Regardless, it was nice to hear her voice after what felt like an eternity.

"M-morning Jaya! We're Viral-X free! Yes, I'm with Nanu now. He's doing okay. I wanted to let you know. I hope you're well!" I fake the energy while sitting up straight in involuntary respect.

"Wake up, sleepyhead! How's Nanu keeping?"

"So far, so good. Still has a cough and shortness of breath, but we can be with him now, so that's a big thing."

"I'm so glad to hear it. He's a fighter...you take after him, you know."

I rub my eyes. I have no idea where that came from or even if it were true, but I hope it is.

"Hmm...you're missed around here, kiddo. I assume you haven't been checking your emails. Your idea got through!"

Oh no, no, *noooo*......

"Err...." I started to protest to stop her right there, but Jaya continued full steam.

"The beverage, Nanki! They are changing the composition of the drink ... " My heart dropped to the floor.

" ... we've had consecutive con-calls with the team, all heads of departments, and they are so excited with this rebrand, AND ... ." I could hear the exclamations in her sentences. I instinctively look towards Nanu. He was still asleep.

" ... they want you to lead this account! We've got the approvals, the plan is taking shape, and we are raring to go! At this rate, we should be ready for launch by the next quarter ... " Silence.

There. She said it. It was over.

"You understand what that means? I was forty by the time I led my first full-fledged campaign. You've done it! You've skipped the steps and climbed the ranks, my brilliant, brilliant child!"

I sit there, blowing air into my cheeks, dumbstruck. "T-That's so great."

I could sense Jaya confused on the other end of the line. Regardless, she didn't probe further and politely ended the conversation soon after.

I continued to keep my fingers tightly crossed—a habit from high school, to ward off any oncoming bad luck.

Chapter 15

2:15 p.m.

What is success?

As a lull hung upon the cold afternoon several hours and cups of tea later, I wondered how I got into this rat race—one that I'm apparently winning too. I hadn't told anyone yet. About the promotion, I mean. Saying it would make it real, and I wasn't quite ready for that. For now, it could be on pause. A maybe or a maybe not.

River seemed to never have anything better to do than indulge my existential crisis, so that's where I go now.

It is different things to different people.

But mostly, it's having gone a step further today than where you were yesterday.

It is the movement of growth.

Why do we chase it?

We don't ask a rose why it lives to bloom...

You know, at the heart of it, I think it's to belong.

But even further,

I think it is maybe

To win at belonging.

And because that makes absolutely no sense but has also been such a sore point of mine, I ask:

How on earth do you land at that?!

Hahaha, here's how the earth I land on that:

When we grow,

it means we have moved forward and in doing so,

moved closer to reaching our highest potential—one that only we knew the existence of
and therefore are responsible for delivering to the world.
It means there was potential,
there has been momentum,
And there is now succession.

It validates the inner workings of our mind to our own selves.

Stagnation is not natural to any living being.
It is a characteristic trait of only non-living things.
Only a stone sits unmoving.
Ageing is itself motion, and motion is a sign of life.
Stagnation breeds sickness, rotting life and health away.

When people get comfortable in their stagnation,
there will always be a rotting of emotional and mental health.

So, most simply, to succeed is to evolve.
And we chase it because we can't stand to stay stagnant.
Life calls to us to move.

What does that have to do with money?

Nothing at all. Why do you ask?

I laugh. He was most unassuming, this man.

In case you didn't notice, people equate your life's success with professional success and money.

In case you didn't notice, other people's opinions aren't the greatest barometer to live your life by.
Making money is just one skill.
It's a great skill, but it's just one thing to be good at.

Just as someone is great at painting, someone is great at football; someone is great at making money.
...

The conventional connotation of success could fit into a teeny tiny box.

When people grow bigger, they aspire to grow bigger
To actually occupy more space under the sun.

With fame, it is to occupy more space in the minds of other people. With money, it's to occupy more physical space on earth.
That in itself is quite a small thing to aspire for because growth is anything but finite.

Money can also mean a livelihood, freedom, and strength.
It can be wildly empowering, but your chase can only last as long as your motivation does.

Yes, of course. It is a means to an end, not the end itself.
I know that 🙄.

Often, though,

the motivation is just to be more. Like you're 'less' as you are, and that is a never-ending, insatiable hunger.

The need to grow bigger for big's sake
must come from a desolate sense of smallness.

Of not belonging.

Yes, well, and no amount of monetary success
can buy you that inherent sense of prosperity, though.

Trust me, I've tried.

Because that comes from inside.
And if it's an inside job,
then you might as well fix that first.

What can be a bigger failure than monetarily succeeding
yet finding lasting fulfillment elude you?
Then where do you go?

Okay. I'm a lot wiser about what it is not. But um…

Again,
What is success?

Success is whatever it means to you.

It's the intention that makes the difference.
What's common, I guess, is impact.
Whether your vision is to create a lasting impact on your own life, family, society or country,
This is why, in fact, it is important for goodness to succeed.
When goodness succeeds, goodness thrives.

Doesn't this constant need to be in motion breed restlessness, though?

It must, yes, in the absence of consciousness.
Experiencing unease is a precursory, mandatory step towards change.
It presents the greatest opportunity to grow.

However, it isn't about renouncing motion and searching for peace in stagnation. Rather, it is about learning to cultivate a restfulness within motion.
Giving up outward action but indulging it in the mind is only hypocrisy.

As long as it exists within your thoughts,
it exists—as real as the sky and the earth.

Refining one's thoughts—
That's where the work is required.

The actions will take care of themselves.

But that's tricky too: Not even all your thoughts are your own.

Only once your thoughts have been detangled
from others', from social conditioning, from delusions and ego,
do you come upon your own.
Raw, unprocessed, pure.

From there,
I allow the actions to flow unabashedly—
a crystal clear reflection of the mind that thinks it, without any worry of reward or its lack thereof.

Imagine the catastrophe if people gave in to their unprocessed thoughts without a care for social repercussions.

You don't trust humanity much, do you?

😛

No comments.

Do you remember, as a child, when someone tells you that unicorns exist, your only reaction is amazement? Not scepticism.

You are accepting of the wonders of the world, even if you cannot see them.

We were never born to doubt the magic and the unknown of the universe, but we for sure learn it.

So it has to have been—that our natural state of being is that of peace and harmony and curiosity.

That's how we were born, and then we learned conflict, and resistance, and apathy.

You are born trusting everyone around you, and then you learn fear and separation.

What we never had to learn was how to love—but we had to learn to hate.

What does that tell you about nature and nurture? The divinely ordained living vs the societally dictated one?

Our natural state is contentment, and we feel misaligned every time we move away from it.

So, it isn't at all about people reverting to animalistic tendencies in cutting out the external noise.

It is, in fact about returning to human tendencies.

Maybe there's a reason why only hurt people hurt people.

Only resentful people feel the excessive need to confine others to their own limitations.

Only people who have lost their joy would cause pain to others.

Isn't that so heart-breaking? That even at our worst, we fight to belong.

It is so painful to be misaligned with the world around us that
if we cannot mirror the joy in it,
it must mirror the pain in us.
Then, we can fit.

We crave an equilibrium. Our hopeless way of feeling connected with our external environment is to have it look like our internal one. We need to feel one with it.

If the storm inside is stronger than the spring outside, it becomes intolerable.

Instead of becoming one with it, we try to make it one like us.

And isn't energy so infectious?

If you carry agitation and conflict within you,

you can't help but infect those you touch energetically.

And by suffocating the peace around you, you only continue subjecting yourself to even more suffocation, but at least now you're not the only one.

No one wins, but everyone loses equally. That's one kind of equilibrium.

But hey, that can also be true of love and joy.

Shouldn't we change the algorithm, then?

How does one stay within love and joy when one is constantly being pulled in different directions?

That's the game, isn't it?

There's no one right way to do anything, of course.

But the end goal is to have a daily discipline
of staying centred and in your higher life condition by fiercely maintaining energetic hygiene.
Simply put, purify the energy you dwell in and therefore give out, AND be careful of what kinds of energies you welcome in.

Energetic hygiene. Yep, we're on that level of hippie now where we talk in 'energetic hygiene' terms.

Surprisingly, I find the inside of River's mind to be a fascinating place to visit. I imagine it to be painted in eclectic neons.

What about all the energies that just happen to casually exist in my environment,
ruining mine?

Energetic vampires.

I'm thinking of Jeff. Whom are you thinking of?

If you know of them, you can choose to do something about it.

You're not a tree.

Either you can change the interaction, or you can change the connection.

Please don't go around trying to change people.
That is a losing battle.

Also delusional.

So it all starts with becoming conscious of the energetic exchange that you are constantly engaged in.

You can never control how others think and act, but you can choose who and what you engage with.

Be very mindful of the energies you interact regularly with.

Observe what mental state it puts you in after that exposure. Does an encounter raise your vibration and inspire you, or does it drain you or anger you?

Does it lift you up and make you feel lighter, or does it feel like an emotional battering?

Whatever their energy, it will rub off on you.

How it makes you feel will stay with you long after they are gone.

Become aware of these experiences and the people in them. Their voices become the voices inside your head—and before you know it, they become your own.
It could drive you crazy if you aren't vigilant.

Let's say I am cool enough to achieve that level of zen.
The absence of negativity isn't always positivity though.
It's a boring neutral sometimes.
How does one rise up from there into happiness?

By choosing to.

Oh, I'm choosing it alright.

And by being disciplined about that choice.

Dammit. You lost me there.

To not get pulled out of your contentment and sense of peace by situations, people, and external forces demands discipline and conscious effort.

This is true for both the presence of problematic triggers and the absence of exciting ones.

They are all just vehicles to take you home anyway—none of them are the destination.

It takes reconnecting with your 'self' energy daily.

Creating pockets of routine every day that strengthen and celebrate it.

For some, that may be prayer, chanting, meditation...whatever else have you.

It's your emotional gym, I guess.

Just like organising the home button on your mobile phone: All other apps simply exist in it ☺

I let the light-heartedness of the chat take over.

What do these saintly, consciously happy people look like, please?

I'm partly amused and partly curious about what he thinks of that.

Hahaha, well historically,

We've always painted enlightened people as having a halo, haven't we?

Maybe, in reality, it isn't an external light shining around them,

it is their internal light burning bright from within them. Ironically, they are the ones who make life look effortless.

Joyful, breezy, and worth the journey. A privilege, even. But as we all find out, eventually, effortlessness takes the most effort of all.

They could fool you into thinking that they've just had it better when, in reality,
they've just lived it better—and it shows.

What about the things they lose along the way?
Because everyone must have.

Exactly, no?
Everyone must have. So, it must be
that people who are successful at cultivating lasting happiness in their lives act from a place of peaceful detachment because they do not need external joys.

Everyone enjoys them, and I'm sure there is suffering upon loss.

But they don't need it. Not at all.

Their joy springs from within them, and so is in abundance.

They can then carry it, unadulterated, into their environments.

As a joyful responsibility to deliver the liveliness of their life for the aliveness of the world.

Time is a mental limitation. An illusion.

A human way of bookending a scary infinity
by breaking it down into small pockets that we can understand
and engage with
and exist within.

It's fascinating, isn't it?

How the universe, though, is far too infinite to exist in time,
but rather time exists within it.

Why put so much value on success and attach so much pain to failure, then?

When you aren't trying so hard to find a predetermined pattern and actually seeing,

as an observer, the nuances of the world and your life in it,
you may arrive upon a far more authentic living.

Hahahhaha, so what

your solution is to leave all jobs and become a Bungy jumper?

Preferably. 😅
But where that's not possible,

to simply carry the spirit of the Bungy jumper into every day would do just fine.

What a relentless salesman!

And what does that spirit look like?

One that knows

that life is in the moments.

It's the greatest learning from the edge:
that it's always going to be your relationship with yourself that counts in the end.

Stay above the negativity.

Don't cut down the life in your years by getting drawn
into another's inner drama

If someone is out of alignment with their natural state of being

of love and peace and unconditional acceptance,
let them not take you with them,
but nor should you need to shake them out of it.

Just let the light within you burn stronger
than the darkness within them.

The one that weighs more wins and consumes the other.

Ahem, sure. Jeff can have his journey to un-stupidify himself.

I look up at Nanu, who sat snuggled in the living room, swathed in his shawl, watching the news on television. He had definitely diminished in the space he occupied. Looking at his frail frame now, I notice how blissful he looked, regardless. A freshly ironed kurta again today. I know this was his way of expressing gratitude for having made it. He was thanking the day for coming in and not having given up on him. He was welcoming it with open arms.

Oh, Nanu has always been a happy man, but he dressed up for these simple pleasures now like they were his biggest blessings. Some days, *success* looks like having made it to the living room from the bedroom, and some days, that can amount to infinitely more than leading an international brand account in the most successful MNC* of the country.

How can you tell the difference?

Between if you're motivated by greed or by passion?

Oh, that is the simplest thing in the world:

It is the difference between doing things for love
—and from love.

And somewhere within that journey lies all of our morality and evolution.

It is as simple and as difficult as that.

And that was everything I needed to know.

For love or *from* love.

But that's not all. I knew what I needed to do.

That evening, I gave myself the permission to entertain what I had been swatting away for lack of it making any perceivable sense. This time, it wasn't impulsive. With fierce mindfulness, I googled the contact details of something that had taken refuge in my head since a random encounter in the wee hours of a December morning—

A little group of people called Dharma Foundation.

Chapter 16

How is it a new year already when my body is still aching like it is living a very old life? For New Year's Eve, Rithvik and I snuck out for a drive under the moon, like we used to. It was his idea, of course; he's the one that brings adventure to this relationship. While I would've—and was—paranoid for Nanu's sake, I'm feeling the wild recklessness of wanting to take chances while I can. I don't think he was expecting me to say yes, and the way his face lit up when I did makes me sad for him.

"This is nice, right?" he had said.

I had smiled. That was my conversation on the one moonlit drive we took in a year. I wish I had more to say. But it was nice, so what else was there to add?

The streets had been eerily empty.

He had a genius brainwave of driving through all our favourite places.

"First of all, everything's going to be shut. Second of all, police?"

Reason. That's what I bring to this relationship. The roads were being manned by cops to ensure the lockdown was observed. He gave me a mischievous smile and said, "I have ways," and zoomed off through the most obscure off-roads and by-lanes to cross through Nirula's, Lodhi Gardens, and India Gate. Don't ask me how we managed to avoid cops. I still don't know. In a way, we were chasing ghosts—the places we loved were down to their skeletons, but I didn't hate it at all. They were still made of the stories we lived and held the promise of better days to come. We finally found things to talk about. In fact, I don't remember shutting up after that. Anyway, that was our New Year's.

In other news, Nanu is definitely still grappling. It had been almost half a month since he had tested positive and four days since he had stepped out of isolation. As I sit in the living room, chopping *bhindi* for dinner today, I watch him keenly.

There was a perpetual wheeze now. His breathing was tedious, his appetite wasn't the same, and his body moved with a new tiredness.

While I was deliberately focussing on counting the milestones and basking in the progress, there was no hiding from it: it was not yet behind us. At this point, it really feels like we're racing down an accident-prone road, terrifyingly fast to just get out, decidedly not looking back or around at any collateral damage. Just as long as I make it to the other end. I feel weirdly responsible. There is this ridiculous, lingering guilt at having invited the work call in. To make up for it, I'm spending an equally ridiculous amount of time these days scouring the internet for all the hacks to beat what damage the virus had left behind. Almost obsessively so. In the hopes that ridiculous nullifies ridiculous somehow.

So we sit in the sun by eleven am every day, sucking on a citrus fruit. Something to do with Vitamin C boosting immunity. We switched over to drinking warm water from copper pots all day instead of our usual refrigerated plastic bottles of water. 'Delete the toxins out of your life,' a popular wise man on T.V. had said. I wasn't sure of his credentials; all he did was *be wise.* Doesn't take much to be that these days.

We take an online Yoga meditation class every day. A calm, harmonious, and happy mind was the best protection one could get, they said. For eight thousand rupees a month, I'm very much counting on it.

We added into our nightly routine what my grandmother used to call a Kadha. A traditional Ayurvedic recipe passed down from generation to generation in India as a shield against all cold and sore throat-related symptoms. I had to ask mum for the recipe, who was overtly enthused at providing it. I think she has some lingering mom guilt at 'abandoning' me. Yes, thirty-two-year-old me, but who can rationalise with Indian mums? It was the most disgusting liquid I have ever ingested, just as I remember it, but the whole family seemed to swear by it, so I gulped it down, also just as I remembered to have done. It was a potion made by boiling down herbs, roots, and spices on a low flame for about an hour till it was reduced to a black, syrupy goop. It tasted as bad as it looked, but every time I had it, I could feel the heat of it trickle down to every last cell, warming me from the inside.

Every time it did that, I looked up and said a mental *thank you* to my grandma for coming through for them, even long after she was gone. I hadn't known her too long, and I didn't have a lot of memories either.

Just a couple of passed-down recipes and a ton of warmth. Maybe that's what grandmothers were.

I didn't quite know if any of this was working in the slightest, but what else was there to do other than hope?

There was also another thing, though.

The community WhatsApp group had been circulating a notice for a conference prayer meeting this weekend. Rithvik, as usual, wouldn't even have opened it.

It said that collective prayer had a higher healing frequency on account of the pooling of energy. Since I'm a newly instated expert on that buzzword now, I find myself following that thread. I wonder if God was getting old too. He must be going deaf if he needed to be yelled out to through a telepathic trumpet these days, no?

I would never admit it out loud, but I'm considering joining in. If nothing else, it could be a crash course on how to do this prayer business.

By Saturday morning, Nanu was weaker still. Is it just me, or is he looking like he's getting thinner every day? His cheeks seem sallow.

Rithvik was asleep at six in the morning when I slip out of the bedroom to attend the first prayer meeting being held on Zoom.

We had been given a mantra yesterday that we were to be chanting together. It was a Sanskrit prayer, one I didn't recognise, written in English. Consisting of four extremely long and extremely complicated lines, we were to learn them to chant along.

Their meaning was written in English below, which translated to a praise of the deity, an acknowledgement of the divine power, and a call for protection.

Extremely sceptical, I did it anyway. *Nothing to lose,* I keep telling myself.

There seemed to be more participants than I had anticipated. It starts with a man I don't know. I expected to, only because they're all supposedly from our colony. He's freshly bathed, extremely awake, and unusually motivated, leading the meet.

I feel out of place already.

"*Namaste, suprabhat,* good morning."

This feels like Kaun Banega Crorepati energy.

He continues, "For all those who are new, I'm Keshav Lal, and seeing the overwhelming response today, we, the Malviya Nagar society, are blessing you all by making this a weekly affair!"

Err, okay. It's a hard pill to digest. *Blessing you all?!*

"*Chaliye, shuru karte hain*"

Oh wow, they just jump right into it.

No protocol, no instructions—just sitting in front of the laptop, chanting garbled words into the screen. Okay, then. Feeling like a monkey in a zoo, I just start aping their moves. How others sit, how they enunciate, the intonation, the decibel.

We just chanted and chanted and chanted. Some with folded hands, some with eyes closed, some distracted but mumbling along anyway.

This little circus goes on for an hour. Well, it *was* nice seeing the neighbours after so long. It does feel nice to be part of the community, struggling together and striving together. It definitely is energising to be sitting on the balcony amidst my plants, consciously praying. The idea of it is nice anyway.

But faith? I'm not sure if I feel that, but I'm trying really, really hard to copy that too.

Secretly, I chanted for the next five days. Morning and evening.

Nanu was showing no tangible improvements, and the doctor on call suspected his lungs had been affected. Nanu has been refusing to get any more tests done, saying he was getting by just fine. He drank a lot more tea than usual and seemed to relish it even more slowly. He asked for his favourite foods to be made every day even though he barely had an appetite. He asked to be around wherever I was in the house, even though he didn't seem to have much energy to talk. He just sat back, wrapped in his shawl draped over his choicest kurta every day, looking out at the world just blissfully. I wonder what on earth he was so blissful about, but he sure made for a pretty sight. He looked content and beautiful. By the sixth day after his 'release' from the isolation, his cough seemed to have taken on an aggressive turn.

3:35 p.m.

Do you believe in God?

I asked River that afternoon, honestly scared and desperate for miracles.

I do

What do you know about Him?

Him. I had no energy to fight this vestige of old sexism right now and gave in to tired submission.

That we will never fully know Him, but we will always be known.

Sounded like the tagline of a creepy murder mystery. God... I try to visualise the concept and fail. I look at the sky through my window instead and ask.

If we ever find ourselves needing to get in touch, how would we start?

By getting in touch with ourselves.

Our life force is the closest divine creation we get access to.

I will never know everything about the world there is to know.

Nor will I ever fully comprehend the infinity of God or the wisdom of the universe.

But I know a little about me.

I find that's enough.
My only real knowledge about the world is my awareness of myself.
So, every new day, I try a little harder to know a little more.

That's what I call meditation, and that's my prayer.
I close my eyes and watch as my breath rises and falls, like the sun, the moon, the day, the night—the life.

I come to the consciousness of God moving through me, as life, and I simply observe his art in motion through my being.

I acknowledge, I appreciate and so, I harness.

In turning inward, in honouring myself, I let myself become an instrument for Godliness to flow through,

unobstructed even by me—
That is my way of devotion.

I fall silent.

What brings you to this question today?

My grandfather...
I don't want to lose him.

Aah, ma chèrie.

You could never lose him.

We could never own people, even if we desperately wanted to.

So we don't even **have** them in the first place—nor do we even hold them briefly.

We just share time.

Heart-breaking and heart-healing, all at once: *We just share time.*

As the evening rolled around, I decided to skip my chanting session to sit beside Nanu. We sipped on hot masala chai with Parle-G glucose biscuits. It was tradition to dunk them into the tea, scramble to eat a bite before the rest caved in the moment it touched the hot liquid, and then follow it up with a generous gulp. By the end, the fallen remnants collected at the bottom of the cup and were dredged out with the glee only a puddle of sugary goodness can bring. Despite the butter Danish cookies becoming a pantry staple now, this was still the epitome of comfort. Those just don't crumble the same.

Nanu had been lying down on the sofa in the living room since morning. Not necessarily asleep, not awake either. The heater had been humming all day long, having stayed on to warm his shawl. The frigid Delhi winter was as unrelenting as every year, Viral-X-no bar. His wheezing had been constant today, and he had had to work much, much harder to draw in the icy cold air into his lungs.

Breath after breath after breath.

It was tiring just listening to him. It was heart-breaking seeing him having to struggle. I think I'm going to be sick from how helpless I feel.

I shut all the doors and windows to keep as much of the cold out as I could. Rithvik had brought out our old shawls and wrapped them around Nanu's feet to keep them warm.

It was only when I brewed some hot ginger tea that he sat up, eager and waiting. Although he is highly diabetic, I can't stop myself from adding the Parle-G he loves so much to his tray today.

I've dabbled with coffee, but after all the lockdowns now, I think I have a new respect for tea. Nothing brings families together in India like chai.

As I sit looking over at him, truly relishing his steaming mug, I move closer. I hold his free hand in mine. He smiles warmly, asks me no questions, and clutches back tighter.

Despite his hands being so wrinkled and weak, it still has the effect of making me feel shielded somehow, protecting me from the world. I was safe here.

I think back to what River had said about communicating with God, and I find myself closing my eyes and watching my breath rise and fall.

Slow down, I hear myself think.

From the fear, the emotions, the helplessness, the denial....

I exhale deeply. With that breath, I let go of what I have been desperately trying to see—or fighting not to see. When I inhale, I allow myself to see what actually *is*.

I become aware of Nanu's hand in mine, warming even in their cold. I imagine my breath trickling down to my fingertips and into his, reaching within him to feel what he was feeling—if not to lessen his burden, maybe to share it with him, just for a heartbeat.

I don't know if I'm imagining it, but I suddenly felt like I can.

Suddenly, his breath is all I can hear in the room. I'm acutely aware of his presence, and I feel the force of his life—a piece of an infinite God—flowing through him.

Flowing *out* of him. Slowly, steadily, painfully, beautifully.

He knew.

My eyes flew open. I could sense it now, quite inexplicably. He knew, didn't he?

That was why the kurta, the favourite foods, the following me around.

He wasn't welcoming the day in… he was saying goodbye.

Chapter 17

My eyes brim with tears as I watch him sitting bundled up inside his shawls, merrily reaching for another biscuit. It was the first time in the day that he looked remotely close to being comfortable.

I bring my other hand and clasp it over his. My palms grow closer in prayer, clutching his tightly in the middle. I have no time left for my petty insecurities or research on how to reach God. I just bow my head and ask for *help*.

As I turn inwards, the prayer comes to me on its own. Surprisingly, my sincerest prayer didn't ask for stretching out his pained living.

How had I been so selfish…

I couldn't bring myself to keep him around any longer than his health allowed him. Dragging out his days so I didn't have to face his absence—that was not for me to ask for. All I desperately wanted was for him to be well. To not have to suffer anymore.

"Thank you. Just thank you for our time. I got to experience this: his love and his light. Please protect him. I pray for him to be in his highest life condition—whatever that is. Whatever is absolutely the best for him. Please just protect him. Please be there for him. Please be there by him."

As far as prayers go, it was a fairly simple one, really. No rituals, no right way of saying it, not even the right posture, maybe. Yet, in my gut, I knew this was the sincerest prayer I had ever mustered, maybe the sincerest one to have ever existed. Somehow, I knew also, without a doubt, that it had reached its destination. Years later, I would recount this as my first real encounter with faith.

When I opened my eyes, Nanu was downing the last of his tea.

Quite anticlimactic, considering I felt like I had just taken an express tour of heaven and hell and back while he sat here just the same, in our little living room, fishing out the last of his beloved beverage.

We spent the rest of that evening talking about things that mattered. Things that had been left unsaid for no real reason. I told him about my promotion, and he exclaimed and clapped his hands, elated. He smoothed his palm over my head in blessing and told me he'd always be proud of me. That he knows I will achieve whatever I set my heart to.

"That is the problem. Mine just isn't in it anymore," I whispered, almost afraid that reality would hear me before I knew what to do with it.

"Bete, *dil koi kamzor thodi hota hai. Itna bachaa ke chalegi toh sadd jayega*! Hearts are built to weather change. It will survive everything except your own betrayal. When you get to my age, you realise that that's the only betrayal you will never *really* get over... I would never want that life for you," he whispered through rasps.

I showed him where I was starting to see the first signs of ageing on my face and how it scared me. I tilted my face to highlight that one new wrinkle that was beginning to form at the edges of my eyes.

He cupped my face in his palm and said, "Lucky girl! Now you have proof of having smiled long and hard enough for your face to have moulded around its lines. Just like the fold lines that impress themselves permanently upon a fragile piece of paper—a map of where it has been."

I told him about River, and he said, "See, how important it is to surround yourself with good people?"

Yes, I thought, how beautiful that some days goodness is simply sending a picture of a Himalayan mountain to a person on a lonely night, in isolation far, far away from its beauty. Nanu had a reminiscing quality even when talking about his present. "How odd a time to live through, where getting Rishikesh to a person stuck in Delhi can become just as meaningful as bringing water to a person stuck in a parched desert."

Most of all, we spoke about how Godliness can still always be found in the unlikeliest of times and places. We called Mum via video and kept the call going for the entire evening. We enjoyed a virtual dinner together. We had managed a Kofta Curry with rice today. It had taken both Rithvik and my efforts to get it ready. We turned up the volume on his Caravan as we sat to eat.

'*Tera Mujhse hai pehele ka naata koi...*'

Mum put down her spoon on the other end of the line and started singing exuberantly for Nanu.

Rithvik and I followed the suit. '*Yunhi nahi dil lubhaata koi...*'

Nanu smiled his brightest smile and clapped his hands together to the chorus:

'Jaaney tuuuu, yaa jaaney naaaa ...'

That night, we set the mattresses in his room again. We decided to all huddle around together tonight. Our own little sleepover party. I kissed Nanu on his forehead and told him I loved him. He hugged me and told me the same.

Holding his hand, we drifted off to sleep. Nanu never woke up again. Heart-breaking as it was, I knew I had been given the greatest gift someone at this time could ask for: I got to say goodbye. It was a privilege denied to too many people stuck in Viral-X wards, in isolation, in hospital waiting rooms. Families weren't even allowed access to the bodies after death, let alone to cremate them with due respect. People couldn't say goodbye to their children, their spouses, or their parents as they died gasping for air, alone and suffering.

I will always remember that on their behalf. I would always let that fuel me going forward because now I knew what this grief means—of what it does. Getting to say goodbye saved me. I got to tell Nanu how much I loved him by holding his hand even as he slipped through my fingers.

We just share time.

I *got* to share mine—and what a beautiful evening we had made of it.

It had been a befitting farewell.

I look out the window at the busily humming street, tucked cosily within this pocket of Malviya Nagar in Delhi and let the cool January air bathe me. It is a quarter past six, and I am exhausted already. It has been thirteen days since the passing of my maternal grandfather, my Nanu—and the culturally appropriate quarantine for grieving was almost up. This marked the end of the official mourning period, and I still felt completely out of my depth to even begin processing it.

"It is believed that the soul of the deceased hangs around for thirteen days be-be-be-cause it is unable to sever ties with its physical body," Mom had shakily explained on the call, unabashedly breaking into hysterical crying yet again.

She couldn't come from Kodaikanal because travel was still prohibited, particularly for senior citizens. It was a terrible state of affairs, but no more terrible than what was now usual. Oh, she had loved him so, so much—a love that I had inherited in its entirety.

As per instruction, I patiently waited around the house I grew up in for a sign of his astral presence and looked keenly—I hadn't much taste for traditions, but I didn't negate them entirely either. Honestly, I didn't normally think about them at all. But, if ever there was a moment to believe...

Added to that was the pressure of arranging a virtual funeral, demanding me to strike a healthy balance between conveying gloomy sombreness along with a package of the best pure *ghee laddoos* from 'Haldiram' only, as mum had insisted.

This is how the thirteen days came and went. All the mystic action the house witnessed was how it neatly and surely shrunk him out of existence as if he had been dead for a long time. His rocking chair was packed into the storage, his shawl—always lazily sprawled across the sofa—was folded into the cupboard, and his favourite tea mug now laid idly at the back of the pantry. *Traitors.*

His Caravan music box lay mute and grieving, a solemn receptacle for the dust of the days. This one hurt me the most. It's like he took the music of our home with him, and now it lay cold and bare and hurting.

The last shaft of sunlight that lit the room with dust speckling through was dimming now. The sun was starting to set, and it was the part of the day where it was no more evening but not quite night yet. The dreaded twilight. Dark but not dark enough, light but barely-lit. How I hated this part of the day, never knowing what quite to do with myself at this hour. I don't even have Nanu to make chai for.

I dust Nanu's books and stack them neatly back onto the shelf. The pile to be discarded lay scattered on the floor. His clothes had been folded neatly after keeping aside the shirts that Rithvik could use. His medicines, cane, and stationery lay in cartons, all set aside to be donated to relevant places. Nanu's whole life lay wrapped in a few boxes at her feet. I go to my Instagram page to find a good photo of his and see my own profile from a stranger's perspective. I trace the clues that laid out the map of my life to anyone who looked: At happy photos, at exquisite souvenirs collected from numerous travels, at shiny awards, at all the signs of the life I had made for myself. At friends, travels, and family reunions. My life, as clearly laid out by the gram.

The journey between building these tiny boxes and being packed up into the ones that lay at my feet was not that long and just frankly underwhelming—and *that* was overwhelming. I wonder again if this is all there will ever be. Evil, *evil* voice. That black dot. A rip in my fabric of contentment. I could feel it now, knocking. It was a feeling of a… certain lack. See, the Mehtas are mighty good at handling loss. Even after all these years, I've always felt like the younger daughter of our family. The ghost of my elder sister may just as well have been the loudest member of our family. But don't go feeling bad for us. Most families I know wrap themselves around a ghost of something that sits large in their living room.

All the things that are never said but always felt. What haunts me is how, down the generations, they continue to find newer ways to feel the same old pain. Family lines cursed with a wound that just won't fill. I look at Rithvik pacing the hallway on his quarterly call with his parents. I think about how I'm infected with mine: how we lose things and live with that loss forever. That is familiar. But to have them? That is the challenge. I wouldn't know where to begin with how to go about that.

I type furiously to River:

6:15 p.m.

How do you feel a lack? How do you feel a void? Numbness is supposed to be just...numb—unfeeling and quiet.

Yet, it is the noisiest feeling in the world!

I look back at my years splayed out in pictures. My pretty little life. Insta-sized, filtered just right, decorated with a bow. It's a lot. And yet, it isn't nearly enough. Maybe, happily-ever-after is boring, I conclude.

River is typing…

After a moment of me hanging onto my phone, he writes one line in response to my existential crisis. *One.*

Why is it that people who are so used to the noise
of every day,
just wither when forced to listen to silence?

I narrow my eyes and pull a face.

Why is it that you answer questions with even more questions?

Most answers lie in asking the right questions!

Do they not?

I roll my eyes and throw my phone aside. His wit is not welcome at this ungodly hour.

I allow myself a deep sigh and let the burdens of the day, the fortnight, the life fall over me as I soak in the city: noisy, overcrowded, buzzing. Alive. I loved it—and I couldn't stand it a second longer.

I go about the next two weeks rather mutely. Then something just cracks. Finally and completely. Almost as if from the outside, I see myself pack a bag and leave for Rishikesh.

Chapter 18

Would I call it a meltdown? Probably. It came *upon* me, is what it was. In some part of my mind, it had already been happening, I think. I just got up from dinner, determinedly *done* with this charade, and just started scurrying around the house, packing a duffel bag and a small suitcase. I must've looked like a mad woman to Rithvik. I sure felt like one. His gaze followed me around the house like I was possessed. I probably was. By that girl hidden deep inside the closet of odds, maybe. I had never travelled anywhere alone. Not without a purpose, anyway. Which is why the last month had felt like a build-up to this point. Rithvik, despite grieving himself, made those funny-looking googly eyes that scour for some sense in a situation. I could give him none.

"B-but why. . . ." He was genuinely bewildered. His hair was scruffy, and he was due for a shave.

I had no answer, just a tangible determination. So strong-willed it was that it emanated out of me like an odd kind of defiance. The kind that let him know this was happening, regardless of how he felt about it. In such an unknown territory he seemed to be that he agreed to go along with whatever was coming because it was all alien.

"I'm coming with you," he declared.

"Why?" I was calm as a cucumber. "B-because ... !"

There was no end to that sentence, just utter flabbergastion. "Because what?"

"Because I'm here! B-because you can't go alone!"

In our first year of going from friends to a couple, he would whip out his husband-behaviour toolkit and would do these random acts to protect me, like moving towards the traffic side of the road while walking. It made me feel delicate. It made me feel like a woman—*his* woman.

It felt like a claim to the world that I was his to safeguard. It probably still would. It's not his fault that right now, it's making me feel suffocated. I wasn't *actually* in need of any protection. It had taken me a few years to realise that, but I had learned to love my strength. Why won't he be proud of that instead? It had taken me so much to get here after all. I know he feels this is what it is to 'be there for me' and has dutifully extended that emotion, Neanderthal-ish though it was. As we grow older, however, his 'care' will just have to look differently.

We were both equally capable which should mean that we both protect each other, we both nurture each other, and we both allow each other to grow as individuals—even if that means letting our partnership take a backseat for a little bit.

"Why not?" I counter.

"I mean... you'll at least need me to handle things," he's sputtering the words out.

"What things?"

"... Nanki!"

Patriarchy had really done a number on men too, hadn't it? What would it take for them to realise that they weren't what's keeping the world together? That they weren't needed at every step, that their permission wasn't asked for.

"Rithvik," I glare right back.

"You can't just go off alone ... " He was repeating himself now, with no rational argument left to make.

"Of course I can."

"B-but why would you want to?" his voice was getting squeaky. I know this voice. He feels hurt that I would want a moment in my life that didn't include him.

A moment to myself to figure stuff out in my head without anybody else influencing my decision, even if unknowingly. A moment of silence.

"Because I do, Rithvik. That should be reason enough."

He looks at me like I am putting up a wall between us. A wall to keep him out. At a later point, I'm sure I could dredge out a teaspoonful of empathy, but right now, he's frustrating me. My eyes blazed. Could he stop looking like such a wounded puppy? Wanting a little bit of time for myself wasn't the same as cutting him out. What was this guilt I'm being made to feel at prioritising myself? I didn't stop being an individual just because I signed up to be part of a pair, did I? Why do partnerships have to make it so hard to simply exist as a person? An individual breathing, living person! Or should I have to want to do everything with him? Because I don't. This was my journey, and he was not a part of it. Not right now.

If anything, I needed to know where on the road I was, so I could tell him where to meet me! He huffed incoherent sounds and then, in a resigned, eerily cold tone, added, "Let me know if you want me around at all..." So his modus operandi was going to be anger.

Fine, then.

I could be angry too, at the fact that he would be angry.

"I will."

I wanted to take a pair of scissors and chop off his excessively long, unkempt hair. If only he could so much as handle his own grooming before thinking himself capable of handling my life for me...!

The next morning, I was out the door.

I scroll up to where it began. The Instagram post of a wildly excited man, as he threw his arms wide open about to take off from the edge of a dizzyingly high bridge, painted a canary yellow. I didn't see a foreigner in him anymore, not even a stranger.

Just a friend I had never met. A friend who found me when I needed it most. But most importantly, and accidentally, in the way I needed it—with just enough distance to let me breathe. When it had come to needing space, it had been a no-brainer. Rishikesh had been in too many chats and dreams, not to run away to now when I needed a pocket of earth to unravel and heal in. Of course, I was excited to actually meet River and experience his experience of it, but I wasn't going to do that right away. Only when I've earned it. I realise only now that I had never officially responded to that ad. It was a *given* that I wouldn't need to, of course, but for the sake of symbolism, I read the post again:

> Can't wait to experience the world again?
> We've got something you can hold onto!
> Send us your story—why daring to take the last step off the edge is just what you need,
> and we'll gift you the experience of a lifetime:
>
> INDIA'S MOST EXTREME BUNGY!
> In Rishikesh!

I feel a tingle at the prospect of walking into that frame soon enough. In the vein of doing things right, I respond to that ad now as I sit in the cab en route to Rishikesh.

It would take me about five more hours, and my stomach was rumbling already.

12.30 p.m.

> Thank you for giving me a glimpse into something I could look forward to, even while I stayed fraught within the darkest of days.

> It kept me wading through the turbulent waters in more ways than you will ever know.

I am coming to experience the overwhelm of the edge for myself.

See you soon-ish.

The car trudged lazily along a dusty road for another hour before his response arrived into my DM.

You haven't yet answered WHY you want to dare to Bungy.

Hmph... I thought that much emotion would at least get me some brownie points, let alone endless chats of pouring my heart out to him.

Erm, you know I can just buy it, right?

Hahahahha, I do.

But you love to torture yourself, so I know you won't...

Dammit. He was right.

This was my journey with him. He brought me up to this point. I wanted him to be the one that leads me to the end—right up to the edge.

URGH!!

I grumbled even as I typed it. Actually, with that grumbly sound, to which the driver threw me a quizzical look through the rearview mirror and said: *Didi, sab theek hai?*

Haan, haan bhaiya, I say, while thinking why things can't just be easy for once.

It isn't going to be easy.

The first step to finding the answers is to ask the right questions—remember?

It is a mind game, and it IS mental warfare. You need to really want to do this.

I need to know your motivations, your reasons for choosing to enter the battlefield.

I need to know your 'Why'.

You need to know your 'why'.

Is there supposed to be a right answer here?

Never.

Oh, Lord! Fine then. Here goes...

My motivations, I think. I ponder this for a while, revisiting my most overwhelming emotions from the last couple of months as I saw River inch closer to the free fall amidst the lush-green mountains.

A LIVER.

He really was one as he jumped gloriously into the forested valley of Rishikesh.

WHY, I ask myself.

Why did I want to do this that night, and why do I *need* to do this now?

I had no answer when Rithvik asked yesterday, but as I ask myself these questions now, in a more peaceful state of mind, the words come to me rather freely.

I write my response in a draft, read it, and then reread it before hitting send.

Dear River,

You must be right about energy being infectious because seeing that excitement in you, even from so far away, manages to keep me as curious about such excitement today as the day I first laid eyes on this post all those weeks ago. God, has it just been weeks? It feels like a lifetime ago.

Here's my entry in response to your ad.

My grandfather passed on.

It's odd. I've never phrased death like that before.

A couple of months ago, if I had to share this news, I might have written it as 'passed away', as an ending, but I know better now.

I believe better now.

He has passed on from being contained within an ageing vessel

To the infinity, he always belonged to.

For that perspective and for that catharsis, thank you.

As I familiarise myself with death,

I guess...I'm trying to reacquaint with life.

Change is difficult, and far too often, fears win. Courage doesn't feel worth the effort, and growth is exchanged for the status quo and curiosity, for stability.

But I want to know.

It is time. I want to know what I'm made of, I want to face my fears. I want to be able to question them and then I want to see what I choose.

Just as an observer of my own mind, as a keen stranger to myself.

So I can be sure of the person I carry on me.

Hopefully, somewhere along that road, I'll know God. That's a meeting I look forward to. You make faith look beautiful.

I want to know God the way you know God.

For that, I hope you'll help me meet me.
P.S. I'm on my way.

Regards,
Nanki

The sun was starting to set, and the air was getting cooler.

As though on cue, my phone beeped loudly, announcing a message from River. It was just one line, but it made my heart swell.

> Welcome to Rishikesh.

I assumed that to mean I had finally qualified. So much for a freebie.

I smile and shake my head at the wild adventures that await me. The wide concrete roads were tapering off, and narrower streets were taking their place. Street lights were coming on, and the evening clouds were clearly visible in the absence of the Delhi smog, letting me know that I was nearing my destination. I roll my window down and inhale deeply. Ah, pure, unadulterated oxygen! How had I gone so long without it? Wind that has whistled through the mountains of the Himalayas and the trees of its jungles just smell different.

I am finally here!

Chapter 19

It's funny. Time had both seemed to have gone by in a blur and also collapsed entirely. As I get out of my cab at the foot of my camp in Tapovan, I stretch myself and hear my body groan with satisfaction. I scan the bustling street that lay before me. Night had almost fallen, little cafes dotted the landscape, and oh, it was just so nice to see people! Everyday people doing everyday things like all was well. Beautifully mundane, regular life at play. What a sight for sore eyes! It wasn't quiet by any measure, but the noise had a simpler quality to it, like it was being played out in a single file. The honking of the few cars that chugged along, the humdrum buzz from the shops, the grazing cows in the middle of the road, and the faint roar of the Ganga in the backdrop. I am tantalisingly close now, and oh, I can feel her beckoning: the mighty Ganges, in all her splendour. Waiting for no one yet, drawing everyone in any way. It had been three years since I had left Delhi. That's over one hundred and fifty-six weeks of the same walls, the same accidental food, the same news. The same hopes, the same fears, the same dreams. Round and round in maddening circles with no exit in sight.

Phew! What a tough road to have made it out of, and I feel half happy, half empty that I had, at least, made it.

Rithvik would've loved this after the sordid nightmare we've been through together. Now that I'm tasting freedom alone, the guilt snagged at me like a knobby old sweater that is all too old and familiar to know exactly where to tug at. That's the strange thing about people: you can choose to go down a different route without really hating the one you leave behind. That's something I know he doesn't realise right now. Or ever, really. But that also can't be why I stay.

I catch myself ruining a perfectly good moment by getting inside my head. Again. I remind myself of the 'why'. River was right—I would need to hold on tight to this little nugget of introspection.

Earlier in the lockdown, I had missed travelling so much that over a period of time, the desire itself had numbed out to accommodate the new reality. So much so that even while I was on my way here, it hadn't really hit me—such a flight of fancy it seemed to be.

Now here, the dull ache of the weeks, the months, the years to break free from the confines of the house comes alive as I realise the cage was, indeed, behind me.

The sky was mine for the taking.

I checked into my tented camp in the late hours of the evening while the stars created a stunning canopy of their own. There was a little trail leading up to it from the reception. Through the darkening evening, I made my way, dragging my suitcase behind me.

While I had been hastily booking from under the blankets as Rithvik snored softly next to me, I came upon this jungle campsite. Its dreamy pictures captivated me like no other lodging had, with beautifully crafted tents amidst what looked like a meadow out of a fairy tale with wild yellow flowers bursting out of its periphery. The reality was even better if that were ever possible in an overly-filtered and glamorised world.

Here, right in front of me, towering in a mildly cosy fashion, was my stay for the next few days: Tent #09. It was an off-white canvas tent, the size of an entire room, covered by an outstretched awning-like cover. An olive green canvas, roll-up window, and door adorned the entrance. There was a thick polka-dotted fabric on the inside of the roof, adding richly to its rustic vibe. Two little jute chairs stood lazily just outside, perfect for tea time. I'm suddenly so excited that I almost hop, skip, and jump to make my way in. I roll up the 'door' like this is all a prop on a movie set and peek in.

Oh my... *wow*.

Ah, the inside. It evokes the kind of comfort that a steaming mug of hot chocolate does on a winter night.

A yawning bed stands facing me upon a wooden floor, with what must be an attached bathroom at the back. I step in to see a little table to my left with a straight-backed chair, a comfortable sofa behind it and a little cane cupboard at the other corner of the room. The entirety of the room is swathed in ethereal white drapes descending down the marquee. This must be how children feel when they first sit on aeroplanes—sheer curiosity and amazement.

At what point do we, as adults, settle into a pattern of things to repeat instead of chasing the wonders we've never seen and done before? And why, I wonder as I brew myself some hot coffee in the electric kettle. I can't deal with dip-dip sachet tea made of milk powder. I'm also starving, but food will have to wait. I guess I'm way hungrier for soaking up the place. I decide to drink this coffee by the Ganges. It's only a short walk down the back of the campsite, the receptionist had said.

I step outside and can feel the icy air fill my lungs, leaving them finally satiated. My breath is fogging up in front of me as I exhale. I cup my hands around the mug and let its heat warm me as I make my way down. The grass rustles beneath my feet, and the chirping of the crickets was drowning out with every step as the gushing river grew louder and louder until: *Oh my God*—there she is!

It wasn't that I hadn't seen her before, but the mighty Ganga had a way of taking anyone's breath away every single time. You have to have experienced it to know it. If wild abundance had a face, it would be hers. Flowing with the beauty of a woman unafraid of her power, Ganga makes her way through the dense green foliage cascading down along with the mountains that they bedecked, captivating India's heart since the beginning of time. Mesmerised, I inch closer, unable to pull my gaze away. A stairway lined this side of the bank, and I find a spot to sit on where the concrete meets the river. I plop myself down and dunk my feet into the freezing water. Not a great idea, I know.

But just like that, I become a part of her ripples. The coldness of the water running over my feet and the tangible beauty of the Ganges made it impossible for me to be anywhere else but here. I feel very present, very in the moment and outside the maze in my head. Taking a generous sip of my hot coffee, I realise my mental chatter has subsided entirely, and I feel a calm descend over me.

I look at the people around me. To this day, people come here to bathe in this holy water with hopes of washing away all the sins within their lifetime—and in death, to be scattered as ashes for eternal forgiveness and peace.

I pull my woollen stole in tighter around me.

I could see people burning camphor on a leaf with a marigold flower and floating it away into the river, like a rudimentary boat carrying their hopes and prayers. The Indian version of a wish upon a star. All the colours meeting my eyes felt more vivid. *Pundits,* robed in saffron, conducted Pujas in small groups, chanting sacred mantras.

Brightly lit temples lined the banks of the river, playing their own hymns amidst a ringing of holy bells. In a lot of ways, all of Rishikesh felt like the inside of a temple.

Pure, holy, and blissful. I bring my phone out and check for calls and messages; there were none. It's fine, I tell myself and click onto Instagram. Today, the tables would turn.

I click the view in front of me and share a live picture.

6:30 p.m.

From one river to another...

You've reached!!

I told you the mountains would wait for you.

Them—and their rivers—welcome you home.

Welcome you home?! Oh, I could almost cry. I was home, indeed.

I feel oddly nervous about actually meeting him. What if he turned out to be crazy—or worse, ordinary?

Have you ever wanted something so much that you couldn't bear to have it?

Nope, I usually just go in for the freefall 😂

Hahhahaha, quite on brand.

Back when life was normal, I used to spend so much time travelling for work. It was one of my favourite perks of the job.

That it took me to new places or newer parts of old places and I used to live for it!

After a while, you realise places are just places.

Whenever anyone would ask me what my favourite place was,

I'd say the airport!

I never stopped loving that part.

The wait, just before... where it could exist in my mind frozen in perpetual perfection.

It was the anticipation of the travel, the idea of a place—that never got old. Rithvik used to call it the Airport syndrome!

Why, of course! Distance allows the most beautiful illusions.

That is, in equal parts, its most wondrous quality as well as its greatest flaw.

Arriving, on the other hand, forces you to engage with the regularity of reality.

Why do you fear it though?

I dunno.

Maybe the idea that it won't be as good as I expect it to be.

Or maybe that it *will,* I think. I look at the mountains that remain hidden within the night. I had waited so long to see them, and I was partly grateful for another night of such a waiting. A dream, once realised, is, after all, over. The more beautiful it is, the worse it is to be done with.

Staying besotted with a dream
may allow you the kind of reliable happiness one can only ever find in dreams,
the reality will always come with the risk of flaws and the possibility of loss.
Living them, however, will allow you to grow in awareness.

What if it isn't everything you thought it to be?

Honestly, it will never be.

And that's why you need to do it so that then you'll know.

That it isn't everything you thought it to be.

That the beauty you imagine is only a projection of the beauty within you.

It is only coming from you—never the view.

So, in that sense, you've been carrying it within you all along.

You just thought you needed an object to project your beauty onto.

Now, you can free yourself from that limitation.

Oh, yuk! 🧀

I rolled my eyes but smiled nonetheless. He wasn't wrong, but was he ever?

I exit the chat, keep the phone aside and for the rest of the evening, I just let Rishikesh happen to me.

The chittering birds delivered the new morning to me.

The night had been cold, my sleep deep, my dreams intense but forgotten already by the time I wake up. It takes me a minute to figure out where I was and I let my mind remind itself gently as I look around and take the surroundings in.

I had no alarms, no calls, no emails, and no plans to get to.

This nothing-to-do was as unusual as it was exciting.

I lay staring at the cascading marquee for a bit. I observe how its fabric folded in and flowed down. I can imagine the city starting to wake up outside of it.

It felt surreal, as if I was still seeing it from a distance. So far away, I had gone within myself over the last year that even though it was behind me now, the heaviness of its months clung to me like a backpack weighed down by rocks. Its darkness still hung like a veil around me. I was here to unpack in more ways than one. I decide it to be so. I get out of bed, put on my fluffy fleece foot warmers, and walk to the door to roll it up. If I had a limited number of hours here, I'd make them count. It was early morning still, and the sun must be out, but I couldn't see it yet. The fog hung low and clouded away any view beyond two feet. Dew perched itself on the wild shrubbery and every blade of grass in sight. In an hour or two, I'd finally be able to see my beloved mountains. Going by the icy coldness of the air I inhale, it feels like Mussoorie in the distance would have had snow. If it did, the peaks could be snow-capped!

An hour later, I sat curled up with a book I had just picked up at the little library in the reception. I was buried deep inside a comforter on one of the jute chairs just outside my tent, lost in its words. When I looked up, the sun was spilling in magnificent beams through the leaves of the trees around me, warming the meadow. The fog had lifted. It was time! I almost trip over the many folds of my shawls, the blankets, and the heavy duvet before I manage to get out. Running into the garden, I look around.

There they were!

The mountains stood tall as ever. Unchanged and majestic. As old as time itself and as strong as youth. No photo in the world, no social media in existence, could remotely capture the essence of actually witnessing their presence—of actually *being* here and seeing it in person.

I really *was* finally here.

Never taking travel for granted again... I mutter under my breath, a promise to myself.

An intense gratitude washes over me to be spared a day to be here—another day to be lived amidst such beauty.

Keenly aware of how many weren't, Nanu included. I look towards the mountains and whisper: *Sorry*...

To an onlooker, it may lack legitimacy, but the mountains knew. We had always shared a language of our own, born of the memories only we were bonded by.

They knew that I was sorry for the years I forgot how much I loved them and for the time I lost in those years to soak up this love.

I was sorry for when I commuted to different places but forgot to truly *travel,* for the curiosity and wonder that had dulled about just how mind-boggling this world is, of how much there is to see and how little time one gets to see it in…

Most importantly, however, and especially in this instant, as I bask in their stoicism, in the knowing that I would forever be as ephemeral to them as a wildflower was to me—I was sorry that I had allowed time to age me. It isn't just them that know me though. I had been right. They were adorned with pristine snow.

Chapter 20

The campsite had arranged for a meditation session. The last time I pushed myself to meditate, it had been an online session during Nanu's recovery. River had mentioned it too, but I hadn't yet experienced the joy he seemed to get out of it.

It's worth a shot, I thought when I signed up. A guru from an Ashram nearby was to come over by 8 a.m. I had been expecting an orange-robed man with his white beard stretching down to his chest. This is why when a middle-aged Indian woman with a nose ring and her hair in a Shiva knot entered, I had to check myself for my mental stereotypes. Oh, and they're blue… I notice as this new-age guru unwrapped her muffler off her head, revealing the punky ends of her hair. She looked like she was in her early forties, with a broad, fit build and a warm face. She sported a fitted black tee and those hippie pants with incantations printed all over them—the kinds one only finds in a place like… well, *here.*

She folded her hands and greeted the class of four people that had gathered there, "Namaste! What a beautiful morning we have here today! I'm Pihu, and I'm a certified Yoga instructor. I will be taking you through a half an hour meditative experience today. So … " she paused to take a look around, "How many of you are doing this for the first time?"

One girl, a teenager by the looks of her, at the back, raised her hand.

"So all others experts then?" Pihu exclaimed, very happy for no apparent reason. I wait for others to talk. So does everyone, apparently. The other two men look around sheepishly, seeming to have forgotten the mechanisms of language.

"Erm … " I chip in, the only real candidate to oblige her here. Even if with an underconfident start on what is a shaky subject for me.

"Yes?" Pihu looked at me warmly, raising her eyebrows and inviting the rest of my words in.

My sense of filter has clearly clogged off late due to inactivity because I say, "Tried it a bit during lockdown, don't understand it fully, don't exactly get the hype."

Oh, God.

"What a wonderful reason to join us today, then!" Pihu beamed, and if it were possible, looked even more excited at the possibilities she presented. I like such people. People who don't get offended easily. Those who lead with curiosity rather than judgment. Makes breathing around them easier. But since that is so rare, had it been any less beaming a face, I would've assumed it to have been sarcasm, but Pihu didn't seem to have that bone. I smile back at her with a growing fondness. Yes, all this before we had even begun. It's funny how little it takes for that first connection.

"Welcome to our meditation class, everyone! Let's sit down in a comfortable position and start with some breathing exercises."

For the next fifteen minutes, we went through the counts of breathing in and exhaling out in double as many counts. A forceful calm had descended upon the little class now. Rishikesh was good at doing that.

Pihu perked up again: "In Sanskrit, the word '*Prana*' means life energy, or life force, and '*Yama*' means to poise or control. The art of breathing is called *Pranayama*.

"It is the age-old funda of mind over matter—YOU learn to control your breath and master your health.

"Meditation is doing the same dance with your mind. Obviously, for as long as you are alive, you will breathe anyway, but by understanding the rhythm of your breath, controlling it, and disciplining it, you create an equilibrium—a harmonious balance. Similarly, with your mind, your thoughts will run anyway. The goal is not to deny them. It is to be okay with their passing while remaining emotionally detached from them.

"Mind chatter can be maddening if not controlled. Hypothetical arguments, ruminating thoughts, rehashing and trying to rearrange old memories, imagining future scenarios—all of it becomes problematic when they hijack your present moments, when it takes you away from noticing the weather touching your skin, the colour of your neighbour's dress, the conversation at the dinner table. It can become scary, especially when this mind chatter becomes loud and persistent enough to be out of your control.

"We get so caught up in them that we often forget that these thoughts are just thoughts—the potential energy, the seed.

"On their own, they are a mere movie inside your mind! But let it go unchecked, and they can very well wreak havoc.

"Meditation is the tool that allows you to choose which channel you're on and which ones you subscribe to! You choose which of those thoughts are to be made into kinetic energy, flowering that seed into the tree of your life.

"Without that discretion, you'd waste all your water, all your energy, and all your precious breath over watering all the weeds too, unknowingly living out of a messy mind. And trust me, there are way too many of those to a highly intelligent and sensitive device like our minds—it picks up all the lint, the voices, the emotions, and the energies from well beyond your conscious awareness. This is how we sift.

"So, for the next thirty minutes, keep your eyes shut and observe what your mind thinks about when life isn't interfering and let them float past you like clouds. Do not engage, do not process, do not attach to it any of your energy.

"Slowly and with time, as you practice this often enough, you let it lose the strength to draw you in, and you start to gain control over redirecting their flow, even when you aren't meditating."

Had it been an orange-robed man with a white beard stretching down to his chest, there is no chance this would have made sense. Pihu made this ancient practice new enough to be able to relate to. In making it relevant, she made it legible.

Now I felt it. I could feel the opening in my heart to genuinely let this in.

As I shut my eyes, I let myself free. I could feel my heart start to race when triggering thoughts came up. I watched as hypothetical conversations with Rithvik came up, where my arguments were perfect in everything, I hadn't yet in physical reality found the words for them. I felt an anxiety flare up about the decisions I was hoping to make and the roads I would be leaving to make them if I did. I felt terrible about Jeff doing a much better job at *my* job right now—that was an intolerable thought to live with. I would just about get drawn into my thoughts when I would remind myself to detach. I could feel my body relax as my fists unclenched (when had they clenched?).

After what felt like an hour, a cold breeze touched my cheek, reminding me of Nanu's cold hands as he had cupped my face the night before… some memories floated up that lived permanently within the crevices of my mind. Nanu's music filling up the air, the laughter over chai, Rithvik dancing at his door…. then with a jolt, I felt a sense of loss in the pit of my stomach when I thought about going back to a home where Nanu didn't exist anymore. A terrifying thought floated in. Somehow, with Nanu's passing, a glaring question presented itself: if there must be hierarchies of love. Since so much of my sense of 'love' within my marriage was because of Nanu's love for Rithvik and how happy Rithvik had made him, now that he was gone, I wonder if my love would be left crumbling through the gaps his absence left behind. What if my marriage was built on some sort of secondary love?

"Love, relax…"

Pihu whispered into my ear, pulling me out of the labyrinthine maze I found myself lost in within my mind yet again. I must have looked tense. Pihu touched the small of my back, nudging me to sit upright from my now hunched posture. She was right. It was a jungle of weeds in there.

I come back to my tent to see twelve missed calls. Twelve. So Mother Dearest has heard. I call her back, and before I have a chance to say hello, she goes with full intensity, "Arre? Nanki, where are you? What has happened? Oh my God, we are so worried."

I sigh. "Rishikesh," I venture slowly.

"Have you had a fight with Rithvik? He's worried too, beta. I mean, fight if you must, but why can't you fight inside one house? Why do you have to stretch this across two states? That too between a pandemic?"

I sigh again. I'm exhausted already. "Mom. I'm not fighting with Rithvik. I think. This isn't about him."

"Should we come?" she asks pleadingly. I can sense her panic that something is amiss. She always gets like this.

She didn't care much for the rest of the world, but inside 26 Geetanjali enclave, she was single-handedly on a mission to harvest an ideal world where everything was perfect. Like her life depended on it. I played along like it did too.

"No," I say flatly. I've always tried to be what she needs me to be, and it cost me the tools to find my peace. I wonder how differently I'd have turned out if she had managed to find hers.

"Okay. Okay, s-so you want a picnic? I think you've just gotten bored inside the house. It would've been nice if you'd taken Rithvik along..."

"No, it's not a picnic. I'm lost. That happens to people sometimes. It's okay. I'll find my way somehow."

"B-but that could be any number of days ... "

"Yes, Mom. Life is uncertain. What can we do about it?"

That's when she started to cry. I did too.

You know, 'The Perfect Child' was probably my masterpiece brand. I became it and sold it every single day. But no. I'm not a wounded child anymore, and I won't live a life that implicates them. I won't live a life that imprisons me. For now, we decided to pause on trying to understand each other. Which I guess is as far as it can go, all things considered.

6:07 p.m.

I failed meditation.

One doesn't fail meditation; one finds their way in it.

Ugh...can we chat like regular peasants for once?

Because I really wanted to do it well today. It was such a beautiful experience.

Early in the day, after I had spent my morning with the mountains with this amazing teacher.

But sitting quietly brought up the worst thoughts,
and before I knew it, I would get entangled within them.

Oh, hey, that is part of the process!

Don't be too hard on yourself.
It takes consistently going into the tangles,
before you learn to organise them.

Yes, it brings up the worst sometimes,
but isn't it good to know what's lurking beneath the surface?

It's the work that's yet to be done.

Yes, I guess.

It is what I'm here to do...
I'm here to make notes of allll the work that's yet to be done.

This is my first time travelling solo btw.

Oh, congratulations!

How is that going for you so far?

I mean, you're never really alone.

The voices in your head keep following you around, so it isn't as peaceful as I thought 😛

Maybe that's why they pulled you away from any others then? So you do not get distracted.

Maybe.

You sound like the kind of person who'd wholly and loudly encourage people to travel solo.

Hahaha, actually, quite the contrary.

I think one should be able to travel alone without descending into a feeling of loneliness.

It inculcates an awareness of our own completeness and enjoyment of that experience.
Ultimately, we're all going to die alone, aren't we? I'd say that's a skill one must have!

But if one needs to, then too, it is a cause for concern.
To fall out of touch with yourself amongst people
is as alarming as not being able to function without them.

That you need to isolate to think and feel and be comfortable means that you are unable to do that in company.

It's like getting sick from the sun.

If this is going to be the case, you're going to be sick a lot.

Ironically, the only way to fix that
is to strengthen your sense of self to such a degree that external stimuli don't influence your ecosystem.
This is your emotional immunity.

Try finding happiness outside
when there are tangles within to be resolved, and you'll always come up empty.

> Keep your insides organised,
> and the outside will not even matter.

If the lockdown had taught me one thing, it was that. You can have everything perfect on paper and still be far from a fairytale happiness. Believe it or not, it wasn't dependent on the prince finding you, or the crown or the castle, because I found myself all those things, and it had still not been enough. Who knew the search for that happiness would take me through meditation, therapeutic chats, and possibly a bungy jump?

Chapter 21

The vaccines had been announced. They had been rolled out a month ago but had only been made accessible to healthcare workers so far—the first responders in this global crisis.

This afternoon, on the little television set in the reception, I saw a reporter standing outside the Ministry of Health in Delhi, announcing that by March, India was ready to start administering the vaccine to its public. It would happen in phases. First to qualify would be the senior citizens and those over the age of forty-five suffering from any comorbidities that left their immunity compromised against the Coronavirus.

Wait! This meant—the parents could get vaccinated soon! This was a little doorway to the exit route. We stood a chance—an actual, real chance to be out of this ... !

I looked on as all the staff of the camp, having stopped mid-track in their chores to listen in, erupted in applause and relief. Who knew what stories they had to tell?

A doctor came on. He was being asked about his experience with the vaccine. Awkwardly, he narrated his flu-like symptoms that started the night after his shot and lasted for a day. He appealed to everyone to get vaccinated, urging them to help reduce the pressure on hospitals amidst the predictions of a second wave.

"If we don't understand the urgency of this now..." he said, straightening his crooked glasses, "our infrastructure could crumble entirely. There will be nothing to save us then."

This was the fastest vaccine in world history to have ever been produced against a virus, and even then, for far too many, it was way too late. It was too late for Nanu.

The doctor seemed acutely aware of it too. He looked like he carried the country's collective exhaustion on his shoulders. The doctors of the world had been the Army of this war.

"Live a life worth the soldier standing guard on the borders, in the line of fire for your safety," Nanu used to say. He had been a part of India's struggle for freedom and never, ever forgot what he gained—what we gained—from the sacrifices of our freedom fighters and soldiers.

The generations to come would also hear of doctors. Of the debt we owe them for risking their lives, safety, and mental sanity to walk into hospitals bursting beyond capacity every single day and through way too many nights. They stood guard amidst torrential death, zipping themselves into suffocating PPE kits to treat the country's most contagious patients for the chance of some more life to save.

For maybe just another night to make it through, maybe so much as just another breath.

A debt that, at the very least, must be worth it if not repaid.

I looked at the clock hanging next to the TV. It ticked at a quarter past three.

It was almost time.

3:35 p.m.

How would I know?

Having rushed back to my room, I was shuffling around, filled with fervent energy, adding layers to my already bulky winter clothing. The meeting with a Mr Kharbanda from Dharma Foundation was scheduled for 4:30 p.m. in the market area. I knew I needed to meet him. What for, I hadn't quite figured yet. I threw in a wad of cash to donate, if nothing else. At least I wouldn't have wasted his time. I feel anxious and tense, realising the incompleteness of my plan only now. The only thing I could think of was to ask River. I didn't quite know how to frame my questions to him a minute before I had to leave, though. I meant to ask him how I would know what to say and do, how to decipher if this was right for me, how I would know if I must, and what value I could possibly bring to the table with my useless skill set in saving the world. I meant to write further while, at the same time, throwing an orange knit scarf around my neck. I was in too much of a flux to type it all. Before I could figure it out, though, River had responded already:

By simply asking.

Without possibly knowing it, he had explained it all.

An auto-rickshaw had been summoned by a waiter at the camp. As I walked towards it, I noticed that there were no security guards and no CCTVs around the property.

Small towns still held a naive trust in people. They still knew each other by name. They still smiled at passerbys. A little world of its own, frozen in another, simpler time.

Okay, so this has been a while, I think, as I climb into the little green rickshaw, its engine already revving. The driver had on a mask, as did I, and from the rear-view mirror, he gestured with his hand to enquire the 'where to' of this journey.

"Lakshman Jhula Market," I say, and off he drove. The dusty road winded downwards, and the auto chugged through it, oddly both rickety and robust at the same time. This is as rudimentary as it gets, and I silently squeal with delight, hidden well under my mask and an unnecessary layer of civilisation. He drops me off at the beginning of the street market for thirty rupees near the barricade; vehicles weren't allowed beyond this point. I hand him a fifty and leave—the lockdown had been terrible for day wagers, especially those depending on the tourism industry. They lived hand-to-mouth as is and suddenly had no income. It was perplexing to think of how they managed. The shops lining the road weren't exactly stalls. Some had brick-and-mortar shops behind the open displays out on the road. The sellers stood outside, lazily inviting walkers in. I wanted to just walk around exploring, but I had somewhere to be. The shops would have to wait. A short walk in stood a sudden clearing around a circle, with a 'no parking' sign plastered on the fence. So obviously, that's where all bikes and two-wheelers were, in blatant rebellion.

Despite that, this stop was iconic. Within the circle stood the tall statue of Lord Lakshman, towering over the area named after him, encased in glass. The crossbow in his hand, the pack of arrows on his back, his royal yellow dhoti, the Rudraksha beads tying his hair into a knot and his chest inflated with pride—just as I remembered it. Iconic in its simplicity. Even though I should hurry, I couldn't help but stop a second longer to admire it. I pull my muffler in nervously. It's getting chillier, and I realise with a jolt that this was the first time ever that I was seeing it without family.

If only I could see it a little more, on their behalf.... to trap this feeling in little gift boxes to carry back to them... I check my phone. It reads 4:12 p.m. It was supposed to be here somewhere. I look around and spot the landmark he had mentioned. '*Pooja Bhandaar*', a little store of religious supplies, stood at the back-right corner of the statue. A narrow road slipped past it, very missable if one didn't know to look for it. I walk down it till I come upon the cafe tucked away to the left. A chalkboard stand outside announced its name: '*Chai Library*'. It's a sign to me that I'm on the right path.

Wow, mum, stop talking in my ear, I think at that thought, grin, and enter. I walk closer to the salon with exposed bricks and an olive-green doorway. I push it open. A door chime tinkers above as I do, and the smell of masala chai and freshly baked sweet buns hits me as it wafts thickly through the air.

I look around. He wasn't here yet. The only light in here comes from low-hanging yellow bulbs. The counter stood right opposite me, with the wall behind it covered in blackboard, listing out at least fifty types of teas in white chalk, with 'MASALA CHAI' standing out in orange. Had to have a place of privilege, this OG. This place had no view, and it didn't bother with it. They converted the linear space to the left of the counter into a corridor library with floor-to-ceiling bookshelves running across the back wall and tables of two set across. The dim lighting and the wooden-panelled floors lent it the vibe of an almost-boudoir, save for the smell of whiskey and some jazz in the background. Instead, there were low Rishikesh hymns and the smell of chai, and somehow, it would seem that this worked just as well.

I ask for some water and wait. Another fifteen minutes must have passed before the door tinkered once more, and a black-turbaned man walked through it. He had on a mask, so it was hard to tell if it was the one who matched the WhatsApp DP of his contact card. Familiar with his way around, he looked to the corridor and, upon spotting me, made his way to the table.

"Namaste-ji. Nanki Mehta?" folding his hands, he enquired. I stood up and nodded, folding my hands to greet him just the same. He was a tall, stately man, looking to be in his sixties, dressed formally, in a coat and everything. He gestured for me to sit down and, thankfully, started, "Bete, first, what will you have?"

Bete, meaning child. It had been a couple of weeks since I had been called that endearment—since Nanu, to be precise—and I feel irrationally overwhelmed. I clear my throat to pace myself and say: "I-I was thinking of trying their nettle tea. I have never heard of it."

"Oh, you know there's a place here where they make soup out of stinging nettles too!" There is a twinkle in his eyes and a bounding, wondrous joy in his deep voice.

"Oh, that sounds absolutely bizarre. I think I want to try it!" I replied as he took his mask off, revealing a kind face, mostly covered in a greying beard and a moustache that curled up at the edges. He placed the order, with a *kulhad* chai for himself and a plate of onion pakoras and mini samosas for the table. I feel childlike in his company.

He clasped his hands on the table and looked me directly in the eye. "Yes, so. How may I be of help to you?"

"Sir, I just wanted to thank you for the tremendous work you've done during the pandemic. We could save a member in our neighbourhood only because of the tireless work of one of your employees. I don't think there are enough words to cover it..." My words feel small.

He folded his hands again. "God must be happy with us to have worked through us, bete. Thank you for letting me know."

"I was wondering..." I began, unsure of where to take it. "Like, what is your process? What is it that you do, and how can others be a part of it?"

"Yes, of course! I am Veer Kharbanda. I started this organisation, Dharma Foundation, about a decade ago.

"We started very small. Just got some children from our colony to volunteer to collect leftover food from the houses to distribute among street kids. We wanted to inculcate an awareness among them of what they can do with their privilege and, of course, have a responsible way of consuming our resources instead of just throwing them away while so many slept hungry. The food could not be half-eaten, stale, or rotten in any way. It was fresh food that had gone untouched. The children went up to every house to collect it, carrying disposable boxes to pack it in, and then walked through to the market area, distributing it to the needy.

"Eventually, families started waiting for the kids to show up. Some prepared food specially to give to them—even sweets around festivals! It was a very enriching experience for everyone involved, but it petered out when exam time came around, and we had to stop.

"Our gated community, however, had gained some momentum. A couple of us families put our heads together and decided to register ourselves as an NGO*. I took charge of the planning and handled it thereon. At the time, I was working a job with a few years left for retirement. After that, this became my full-time thing—Ah, yes."

Our order had arrived. My steaming water-based green leaf tea in a white mug, his saffron spiced milk tea in an earthen kulhad. The piping-hot snacks came on a wooden platter. I picked one bite-sized *samosa* and looked at him to go on.

"These are a specialty here." He smiled as I took a small bite. Freshly out of the fryer, burning hot inside, and lip-smacking, these samosas were truly exceptional. With spicy mashed potatoes and... raisins? What a weird, weird combination. Perfection, actually.

He smiled at my befuddlement and went on.

"Our core team is still four members from our neighbour families from back then."

"Just four?" This was surprising. They had been all over the media, doing so much work during the pandemic, with pictures showing groups of helpers wearing black tees with 'Dharma' printed over them. I had imagined it to be a full-fledged organisation.

"Yes, actually. The others are volunteers. While we have some ardent volunteers who provide us with almost stable service, only four are permanent 'employees' within the organisation. Others come and go as their time and will permits. We started by putting in our own money, but to scale up, we rely on donations. Every contribution goes a long way, but they are wavering. Most NGOs depend heavily on this erraticism as their main source of man and money power. It's what keeps us in existence. However, it isn't always stable. Barely ever, in fact."

"That must be difficult ... " I had come here thinking how I could eat a piece of their altruistic cake. What I could learn about baking it and what I could take away. Instead, I came upon another realisation rather quickly: It hadn't struck me that they could need help. Who ever thinks about the givers? They are already ample enough to be giving unconditionally. What could they possibly be given to?

Maybe that's how they're the first ones to starve.

"Yes, it is. When we started this, our hearts were full, and we thought we could run on its fumes. That's both the beauty and folly of youth.

"We were neither entirely wrong nor right; just incomplete in our understanding. We did run on its fumes, but there's only so far one can go without fuel. No matter how much you do, there's always more to be done. We had to get smart about what we were capable of and accept that which we weren't.

"Over a period of time, however, while our hearts remain just as full, there is this keen awareness that one can't depend entirely on passion. In fact, the most aware of this fact will be the people who have tried to. It needs consistency, direction, and means to become a breathing, living entity."

I winced suddenly in disgust. I had taken a swig of my nettle tea, and it tasted a lot like ... spinach.

"Don't know what I was expecting," I explained as he stopped talking suddenly, startled, "but it wasn't that!"

He threw his head back and roared with laughter. "What else will you have, bete?"

I looked down at my cup. It was just a few more sips of terrible tea. "Oh, it's fine, Sir ..."

"Nonsense! Life is too short for 'fine'. Never settle for anything less than spectacular!" He motioned the waiter to the table.

It must be the mountains, I think, that didn't just stop at making poets out of everyone—it made poetry out of its people too.

"Okay then, I'll have what you're having," and another kulhad chai was ordered ...

I take out my notepad and dashed some bullet points onto it.

- manpower
- money
- stability

"We officially started with free tuition for underprivileged children. They didn't go to school, and a lot of them didn't even want to. It was a waste to them. They needed to earn.

"So, we started with teaching them to simply read and write. Slowly, it grew into a small learning centre where we teach them life skills they can use for vocations that don't require a qualification; we run that to this day, but most of our notable work was actually ad hoc; we would extend ourselves during any crisis we could help with. Like the Kerala floods, the Rishikesh landslides, Bihar earthquakes, and now Viral-X.

"We had made a good name for ourselves within our locality, and they would trust us with diverting their donations. The wonderful thing was, during such disaster management initiatives, our students from our learning centre, and even their older family members were more than willing to take the training to volunteer with the relief work on ground. This included a two-day course on first aid and an orientation on the flow of operations that we would organise before dispatching them to the hit zones."

What a fitting full circle.

The people who received kindness were the first ones to volunteer to give it because they knew what that meant. River was right—energy was infectious. No wonder people treat people the way they have been treated.

Hurt people hurt people; loved people love people. It was so important, then, for those well-loved to reach out to others with the love inevitably contained within them. They have this precious, precious currency that way too many are empty of. It's one thing to sit in your corner and be a kind person when spoken to, it's another to go out there and give it. All that love bottled up inside does no good to the world, does it? If only one could find it in themselves to start that domino effect. "So, you have no singular mission?" Branding-wise, this made them weak, a lack of a USP.

"Just to give what we can. Is that not singular enough?" He had a twinkle in his eye.

I smiled back. It should be.

"Our mission, like people and life, isn't two-dimensional. Its richness lies in its complexities. It holds layers and, like water, flows where it needs to."

"Beyond your locality, how do people know of you? Like during Viral-X, you were huge. In the papers, on social media, and everything. I actually thought your NGO only catered to providing oxygen cylinders. I had no "idea of the amount of work that you have accomplished in the past. How did you manage that when it hasn't been your forte?"

"That's simple. It isn't because we were experts. It's because we were there. Showing up when people were desperate. Times were tough, and no one had the luxury of choice or time. You know, it is the easiest to get volunteers and donations during a crisis.

"Visible misery sells fast. We genuinely were never wanting for money or workers during that period—we had an abundance of both. People were wanting, even desperate, to help because we were all suffering. Nothing binds people together more than common pain.

"We were restricted by a genuine shortage of resources, as was everyone. We were merely trying to organise its flow of operations in the best way possible to optimise it. It's when it is not an emergency that we have trouble running the show. Misery still exists. It's just not urgent enough nor visible enough to be tended to."

I scribble into my book:

- Visible misery
- sustainability.

How does one make passive pain be *felt* consistently enough to inspire sustainable support? It is natural to numb out anything that is too consistent. How is pain kept fresh and alive?

"In Sikhism, we believe in '*Dasvandh*'—that is setting aside one-tenth of our income and… life energy towards Seva. In my experience, everyone wants to contribute. They want to help. The loss, more than in a lack of means, lies in passivity. It's only in times of need that people sit up and take stock of what is needed and appreciate and support the givers. Otherwise, it's taken for granted, unnecessary even. Our spirits must never tire of action. What would be the difference between being alive or not, then?"

The darkness was growing outside, but I feel comforted by his light. I think I had all the answers I needed to finally begin with asking the right questions. For now, we simply enjoy the rest of our tea, and I thank him for his time.

Before we leave, I blurt out, "Why did you agree to meet me?"

I really couldn't help myself.

After all, it had just been a call over a month ago enquiring generally and then one more, to Mr Kharbanda directly, this time, a day before I left for Rishikesh, scheduling the day and time. All I'd said was that I wanted to thank him for saving a life that had mattered to me. That I would love to know more about what they do. There was nothing he stood to get out of his time with me, and yet, unhesitatingly, he had agreed.

On their website, they had listed their locations as Gurugram, Chandigarh, Jaipur, and Rishikesh. I had called and asked to meet their Rishikesh team. It turned out the founder *was* the Rishikesh team, and he visited often on account of his son working in a rafting company here. Delhi was listed as their head office, but I didn't want to meet them there. It was a different segment in my mind, a different life that demanded a different version of me.

Here? Now, here, I could be born again. I could choose to be whomever I wanted to be.

Mr Kharbanda paused before he answered, "Because I sensed something in you."

"What was that?" I tilted my head, waiting.

"A seed... and an urgency to break out of it."

Yep, I thought as we stepped out into the cold yet again and watched him walk away.

Ridiculous optimists, that's what saves the world in the end.

Chapter 22

It had been three days of glossing over the notes from my meeting with Mr Kharbanda. I stared at the same bullet points until a solution, an idea, or a picture started to form out of them, but it was one I was bent on suppressing. This was harder than I had imagined. It was all I could see, and had no more sight to spare.

It came from who I had been, a version I was trying not to be anymore, and that just won't do.

This evening, I sat with the same notepad over a bonfire that the camp put up every night on our lawns, the pencil poised over the paper, waiting. I wasn't writing what was coming to me, and different, just... wasn't.

The teenage girl from my Yoga class was sprawled on the hammock across from me, as she was every other evening, with her headphones on and music seeping out of it. Not loud enough to annoy others, but definitely loud enough to burst her own eardrums while staying perpetually glued to the bulky headset. I didn't tell her that, though—I would not cross that bridge into the old-people category. I just wouldn't.

The two other men from the class must have checked out already. They had travelled together from Amritsar, as had been discussed just that morning after our daily meditation session. Now, *those* had been going rather well. The four of us and Pihu had become more comfortable with the silence and with the journey of getting lost in it alone but together. We shared pleasantries and enquired about the wellbeing of those back home and not too much else, each dealing with their own drama, each here for an escape.

I was looking at the twinkling stars for any inspiration when my phone buzzed. It was Jaya.

My immediate reaction was to scrounge for any reason I could use as an excuse later not to pick up right now. I couldn't find one. Reluctantly, I do.

"Hello ... " I started sheepishly. The conversation hadn't even begun, and I was apologetic already. There was no point playing dumb with Jaya: she knew me too well to buy that.

"My dear girl ... " Jaya began curtly. Oops, I was in trouble. I braced myself for impact.

"First, you go missing. I didn't say a thing, assuming you need the break to grieve Nanu. Then I find out from Rithvik that you've taken off to Rishikesh in the middle of a pandemic. Care to explain to me what's going on in that head of yours? Care to explain to him?" I narrowed my eyes. So Rithvik and Jaya had had a chat....

I stayed silent. "Nanki! This is enough. It is not everyone's job to guess your next step. You are accountable to your work, to your husband, and to me. I know times are tough, but they're tough for everybody. Adult up!"

"I'm sorry." My tone was flat. This wasn't a lie, but it was not nearly the whole picture.

"That's it? You were given the opportunity of a *lifetime*—that I'm still stalling for you, by the way. God knows how I'm doing it. God knows how terrible it is looking that the person who is supposed to lead a brand isn't even present during its painstaking creation…"

"Jaya, I'm not going to do it."

Until that point, I hadn't even realised that my mind was so made up.

There was an explosive silence.

"Excuse—WHAT?"

"I'm not doing it," I repeated, surprised at my conviction. And my guts, really. I didn't know if this was a break or if this was a resignation. All I knew was that I had no mental bandwidth to lead an account, much less to be pressured into urgent action because it was due to hit the market in a few months. I was done being obligated to do things I never chose, and I was done being rushed through life at a pace that wasn't my own.

"Why. The hell. Not? Do you think opportunities like these fall from trees? Rithvik is right. You've completely lost your mind."

I stayed silent because there was nothing to say that made any rational sense. Even to me. Except that my heart was elsewhere, and I had to find where it was taking me. That would just have to be enough.

Also, excuse me? Rithvik said what to my boss now? Oh, I'll deal with that later.

Jaya started on a rant, stating everything I knew already, "… You stopped responding to emails…"

I muted myself and let her rant away to her heart's content, holding the phone at a distance so I could hear the fire crackle and breathe without being interrupted.

"... The team is working round the clock because this is such a big account for us ..."

The teenager flung her feet down and sat looking at me. We locked eyes, and she smiled. An anxious feeling passed through me. To allay it, I, while still on mute, mindlessly ask the teenager instead:

"How can you *ever* hear your own thoughts through that?" Oh damn. Okay then, that bridge had officially been burned down.

"I CAN'T! That's the whole point," she yelled over the noise.

Well. That was probably the difference between the pains of growing and the pains of having grown. The former is about shutting up the maddening inner voice for a moment of peace—a desperation to get off the carousel; the latter is the agonising struggle to find it like it is the only thing that could save you from flying off of it. What is common is the desperation to survive the circus.

"... do you have any idea what you're doing, Nanki?" Jaya blasted.

I unmute myself, draw the mobile close to me, and finally speak into it.

"Not a clue."

And for the first time in a really long time, I was okay with that.

It was almost midnight. I don't usually stay up this late here because of the morning meditation sessions. But tonight, I'm furious because of Rithvik. So, he does think, 'I've lost my mind', was it? Because, for once, I'm not exactly playing by the script? Because he doesn't know exactly what I'm thinking? I've always had a keen awareness of how overly nice people are... just sinister. Giving and giving and giving to make the recipient beholden. Till a relationship is forced out of obligation. This sugary niceness weaponised to manipulate and leveraged to hold people hostage. Rithvik is very nice. Very, very nice, and it's always made a point of, one way or another. I know I have my issues, but he does too.

That's not fair, I hear Nanu's voice in my head say.

Isn't it, though? Why on earth else would he stay?

"Slowly, you may now open your eyes... " Pihu stood with her hands on her hips, the sun hanging behind her head like a halo.

It was starting to warm up, if only a tad. I felt a deep peacefulness within me. This was my tenth session in a row, and I feel mighty proud of myself. Meditation was still a struggle, but I looked forward to the journey now. The jungles were rife, but they didn't feel dangerous anymore.

As Pihu started packing up to leave, she left us students to languish as we will. I didn't feel like moving yet. I sat there in a half Padmasana, or the lotus pose, touched my fingers to the blades of the grass, and enjoyed the feel of them. This was an idyllic life, a background of mountains, the sensation of the earth below, and the sound of the gushing Ganga.

"So I don't know if you know… we have the Kumbh Mela coming up in about a month." I looked up from my reverie to see Pihu pensively address the class. The teenager was still here, and another family of four from Dehradun had checked in and joined us today.

"Try as we might, we can't seem to stop it. It is being touted as a 'super spreader'—and boy, that doesn't even begin to cover it. If you all plan to be here long, I would suggest to keep it short of that. Rishikesh and Haridwar will become Viral-X hotspots, and no amount of precaution can really prevent that. The whole country may be hitting into a second wave as it is. You don't want to be locked out of your states and definitely not here with the millions of pilgrims thronging the Ganga for their holy bath."

We shared nervous glances and nodded solemnly.

The Kumbh Mela, a Hindu festival, happened once every twelve years amidst a cycle of places and had an ardent audience of its own. It invited way too many congregations from the farthest ends of the country to take a dip of atonement in consecrated waters for a global pandemic, but as it were, religion in India could not be messed with, least of all with logic.

So, a month. An end date had been served, and a month was as far as I could be here. I had to arrive at the end of my road before the trip came to its end.

An urgency kicked in. I brought out my phone and hopped onto River's DMs.

I started to write and then deleted my messages. I didn't need to have a chat on text anymore. We could meet in person!

9:15 a.m.

Hi River.

I ventured slowly, wondering if he thought of me as friend enough to meet outside of the bridge. So far, he had only been the Jump Master and I, a person with fears. It was, I assumed, natural for him to gravitate towards them and take the time to sort through each one of its shades to lead me up to the point of climax—the edge. After that, I was on my own. But friends? Who knew if he felt that? All I knew for sure was that without his element of friendliness, his guidance would have meant a lot less. It is what made me trust him. Well, this was pretty much the same thing, all meshed into one odd relationship.

Hello Nanki.

You sound like you must be finding your way back into your skin...

Sorry?

Oh, you know.
This is the first time you've said Hi.

Not with thoughts wandering off the edge of the earth,
not with emotions threatening to take you under,
just peacefully present to this moment.
Just... Hi.

Was that true? How could it be?

I guess I am.

Finding my way back into my skin.

Would you care for a coffee while I navigate the rest of the way?

I hope he wouldn't assume it to be a date. *God,* please don't be cheesy.

How about your Bungy jump?

Oh, thank God.

I'm not ready for my jump yet.

I'll arrive at the edge—when I arrive at the edge.
It will have to be soon, before the Kumbh Mela, in fact,
because I must leave by then.

But it isn't now.

There was a moment's pause. Then—

I'm more of a masala chai person.

I laughed out loud.

I know just the place...

Oh, have you tried the nettle tea here?

....And that's my cue to exit this chat, but I send a rolling eyes emoji before I do.

Chapter 23

We were to meet by six-thirty in the evening at Chai Library.

I wandered through the market as the lights started coming on. The street hawkers had tied strings of bulbs to their carts that twinkled magically now. Tantric music of Sanskrit hymns sung in exotic foreign accents clung to the air that carried them along with the smell of incense.

I made my way to the cafe for the second time in less than a week. I feel surprisingly nervous about this one—jittery almost.

For a stranger, he knew too much about me. Now that he was stepping outside my phone texts and becoming a real, living human, I felt uncomfortably … *seen*. I was also, however, excited to see him.

I pushed the door open and entered to the familiar jangling of the door chimes; the dim yellow lights flooding the place looked even brighter in contrast to the darkening evening outside. I looked around—he was already here!

River sat on the farthest table at the end of the library corridor in a big, dark blue jacket, pouring into a hardbound book. Skin almost glowing under his brown dishevelled hair:

this was the face I had imagined all through the lockdown as the face of a LIVER.

I walk slowly up to him. He looks up from his book only when I am just two steps away. For the length of a heartbeat, he had an entirely blank expression. I inhaled sharply as I looked at him; his eyes were a shade of blue one would imagine the bottom of the ocean to be made of, where the light doesn't even go, holding a terrifying calm of its own.

In the next second, as his eyes met mine, his face broke into the widest smile I had ever seen on a human—and he had dimples!

Oh, just so much beauty is lost in translation from reality to the digital, I think, my own smile mirroring his now. He stood up—more like unfurled himself. He was much taller than I had imagined and walked around the table with his hands outstretched for a.... *handshake*. He hunched down ever so slightly to fit into my eye-line and extended a very warm handshake with both his hands clasping mine, which felt more like a formal, courteous version of a hug.

"Namaste, Nanki!" *Oh boy*, I had no idea what his voice sounded like. It was warm as the sun and heavenly accented.

"*Bonsoir*, River!" my voice was a tad squeaky. He chuckled and pulled out a chair for me.

"*Ah alors tu parles français?*" River invited me in playfully as he sat himself down.

"Okay, no. That's all I had." He laughed a laugh that would light up the galaxy.

The next fifteen minutes went by in a blur of nervous chatter. I asked him about his day, and he replied, "The usual! Got a couple of people to Bungy, that is all!"

"Riiiight, the usual."

I pointed at an 'I've Got Guts!!!' badge on his black T-shirt, and he explained, "Oh! Company policy. All our crew who've jumped wear it. We also give it to the jumpers after their Bungy, so hopefully, it will be yours soon! We are seeing fewer people in Rishikesh now that the cases are rising again…" I started easing up. River felt like River again. Not the detached human his physical presence seemed to display, but as my own friend-*ish* person, I had come to think of him as. The waiter came to the table to take our order, and I asked him for recommendations. I decided upon a Butter Tea today, a speciality from the Himalayas. It was, the waiter explained, also known as Gur-Gur Chai, made of tea leaves from Ladakh, yak milk butter, water, and salt.

River, after careful deliberation, picked a Kashmiri Noon Chai—a sweet milk tea brewed with cardamom, salt, and—baking soda?!—which apparently lent it a distinctive pink colour.

I resumed, "This place… is whacky. Lived in India all my life and had no idea we have so many teas".

River let out a sunny chortle. "It's crazy how we numb out to things the more they are in our face—the more you see of it, the lesser you truly *see* it."

I knew he wasn't just talking about the teas. "Well, yeah! But it is how it's designed to be, isn't it? It is vain you know. Like if I was God, I'd design it differently."

"Would you?" He looked bemused but changed tracks and asked, "How are things back home?"

"I don't know," I say. It was an honest answer. He sat back silently, exuding a most calming patience, waiting for me to go on. "Thank God for you though! I don't know how—or why—you were always there, but… it was a lot."

A part of me gagged at this bleeding of emotion again. How it would've disgusted me a few months ago, and even now, I hoped to revert to my default setting.

River shook his head, "Oh pff… I was a workaholic on a forced sabbatical. Rishikesh was on lockdown for most of it, of course. It was no bother. In fact, by looking to me to lend you courage—you allowed me to be a Jump Master, even without my bridge. Who would've thought my profession would take this form?"

Hmmm. That… happened later though. Eventually.

"Why did you start? Why did you allow me into your space? I could've been any creep."

Our teas arrived, and the question hung in the air. The Noon Chai was indeed a pretty mild hue of pink, served in a wide-rimmed glass cup with pistachio flakes and dried rose petal garnishes. River eyed it with a childlike fascination as it was placed in front of him. My Butter Tea came in a floral bowl with jaggery cubes on the side. So far, it looked like regular tea and had no quirky garnishes to talk about. A basket of complimentary sweet buns was placed on the table with a gracious smile by the waiter.

"Oh, what fun!" River exclaimed. The teas were steaming hot, and I cupped my hands around mine.

"Well?" I probed.

River smiled, but his energy shifted. He put his cup down and looked out the window before answering.

"I was returning from the hospital that night. I had lost a friend to Viral-X. I couldn't go to him because they weren't allowing access to bodies of Viral-X patients. So, I drove to where I needed to instead.

Within the mountains, I am home. It was easy to understand that *want* in you because I was there too. I couldn't imagine making it through that without them. It was the least I could do."

My heart dropped to the floor. I realised how little I knew about him, though I still and inexplicably felt sure of knowing the essence of him.

Within the mountains, I am home.

River. He had told me it was a self-chosen stage name. Was this why? The role he embodies as a Jump Master in Rishikesh. I didn't dare ask. I wasn't ready to trade the myth of him just yet.

It didn't even matter, in fact. He was who he chose to be. I only felt gutted for not even having offered a human-to-human connection and making a God of him instead.

"Why didn't you tell me that?" I whispered.

He smiled now, coming back into his own, "Ah, it was too much to get into, I guess. I wished then that I had a pocket of earth that could just pour into me without needing an exchange coz I had nothing to give right then. So I became that to you. When you're that depleted, all you need is to become full of you."

To become 'full of you'—has such a negative connotation in spoken English. Clearly unknowing of it, River said it unhesitatingly. And oh, so beautifully.

Of course, one must become 'full' of themselves. Up to the brim and bursting through the seams. What the hell else are they supposed to be full of?

I sip on my tea. An unusual version of buttery goodness made its way down my throat. It's not overly rich, but it's not really weird, either. This was a warm, cosy blanket in a mug that one snuggles under after a long day out in the cold. I'm finally making the right choices. I plop two cubes of jaggery in because why not?

"Don't you need friends too?" I wish this hadn't been an afterthought. Better late than never.

"I do, and I have them. Why do you ask?"

Ouch. He didn't think of me as his friend but he allowed me my illusion anyway. But we weren't exactly friends, were we? Which just goes to prove that not every meaningful connection has to be a friendship. It's become a term too loosely used now.

"Oh, we need more labels to define human relationships, don't we?"

"Oh, I think we need far less." River smacked his lips, gulping down a generous sip. "Labels limit things."

Yup. In that instant, I decided. Whatever this was, was. Labels or not, it was, as I had said, a lot.

"That's why it works. Thinking of me as different from them is why people trust me with more strength than them. We equalise the things we know. And to think of something as equal is to assume it to suffer from our own failures. Some people are builders in this world. They take any landscape and build it into a new whole. Some people are so whole themselves that they become a function of giving. These are the teachers and the givers. Even at their broken down pieces, they'll still find something to give. Some, like me, are facilitators. We work best by remaining incomplete to the ones we hope to facilitate. So incomplete, in fact, that by filling the gaps in your knowledge, you raise me up to a figment of your own imagination. That's how you see the version you seek. I am nothing. I am simply what you need. So you can become whole again. Which by default makes me everything, but that's an ego trip I'll take another day," he said, winking. After all this time, he was still a stranger, but he was also anything but. I had always known this but hadn't verbalised it in so many words. No point denying it now. It was a terribly kind gift, so I must make the most of it.

"Actually, you're right. And this makes you what… a lowkey therapist?"

"Naww, I'm too underqualified for that. I'm… maybe just the devil's advocate. An argument for another perspective. A Jump Master getting you to jump." His eyes twinkled.

I hold his gaze as I ran my finger around the rim of my cup. Witnessing his mind in person felt like stumbling upon impromptu poetry.

"So. Again. How are things back home?" This time, River was the one probing.

Now, I was willing to venture into this question, for I had no more for him. I looked around me.

Simply choosing to be here because I wanted to, and making it happen felt like a victory. River sat across from me, like a symbol in himself of what lay ahead. It was like a gathering of courage for what was to come. However, the guilt about what it was costing me stayed within me and followed me wherever I went. It came to me in waves, wearing different faces at different times.

I felt at peace right now, and only because I did, did I allow myself to consciously revisit what I had left behind. If only to detangle the various threads that kept my heart in knots, I allow River into the gaps between our messages.

I tell him about Jaya, who had brought me up in my career like a parent does in life. I'm not naive; I understand that it too was an investment that would probably end up bearing no return for her if I followed my heart instead of Jaya's vision.

Then, I conjure up for him the befuddled face of Rithvik, who was trying his hardest to bring everything back to where it was and couldn't fathom why, instead of holding on to our 'normal' after such a nightmare, I would want to let go of it entirely.

Sometimes, I tell River, my guilt held the angelic face of Kavya, which, for some reason in my mind now, was burned with sorrowful tears. That face ... the one that started it all.

Then—and this was difficult—there was the unconditionally loving face of Nanu, who, right up to the end, saw me as the woman I hoped to be.

If I didn't become her, that would be my biggest failure. Possibly the only one that really counted. I look at him, watching me keenly. From the bulb hanging over my head, the ocean in his eyes glistened, mirroring back a reflection. And then there was me. I didn't say that aloud, but he understood. He held my gaze, allowing me a moment to let the weight of that thought tide through. I then tell him about Mr Kharbanda and his inspiring work, our meeting, my inexplicable pull, and my search for answers to questions I was stumbling upon as the days went by.

Surprisingly, this entire monologue took no more than twenty minutes. It is only a little while that can seem to eat up all of life sometimes.

"So, what do you do now?" River asks me.

"Well, that's what I'm yet to figure out... "

"In my experience, when one doesn't know the answers, it's because they're usually trying to guess someone else's. Betraying their instincts, they're caged within someone else's world."

"Okayy... ?" I looked at him for a second and wondered if that was what I'd been doing. I bring out my notepad mindlessly, looking for clues. I was trying to guess others' answers. Rithvik's, Mr Kharbanda's, Jaya's... God's. Trying to imagine what they would deem as the best answers and fight to guess them.

Where I knew I strayed from their best answers, I felt it as an angst in the heart of my chest. But none of their answers matched, of course. In fact, most were conflicting. Caught in the crossfire, my life was becoming a... garble. Oh My God. I think I almost gasped. It was... probably not my emotion at all! Could it be... .that it was the angst I anticipated them to feel and carried it on their behalf, burdening me, weighing me down? And eventually, it was that weight that was distancing me from them all so I could have a moment of lightness. I gather myself. I go over the points again, aloud this time, for River. His fingers lingered on my scribble of 'visible misery', and I explained what Mr Kharbanda had meant—the struggle to keep pain fresh and alive enough to staying hurt. He nodded, and I said, "Humans are too adaptable for their own good."

I picked up one of the sweet buns. Sprinkled with colourful tutti fruitis, it reminded me of childhood.

"Isn't it ironic that it was adaptability—our ability to adjust to our surroundings, modify ourselves to fit into our environment, to grow numb to what is intolerable and painful so we can persist through it—that got us to survive, and ultimately, it will be adaptability that will be the end of us.

"We always found a way to adapt to what was killing us in order to survive when the pain should have been felt instead, for *it* to be okay. That would be the bigger win, and maybe the whole ecosystem would thrive instead of just surviving."

Huh. Wasn't that true?

"What've you thought about it, then?" he asked, gesturing to the notepad.

"Oh, I haven't been a fan of my brain of late," I brushed it off since that was the question I had been both evading and trying to address myself. "I am, in fact," I add mischievously, "here to birth a new one. Isn't that what your edge is for?"

He gave out a hearty laugh before looking down at his now empty cup.

"Ah, the edge ... " He spoke the word slowly and with a lovingness only a poet must evoke for his muse.

"But that would mean you'd have to kill the old one? I'm sure any head has only space for one!"

"Mmm ... that wouldn't be the worst thing in the world," I say with a twinkle in my eye.

"So, losing yourself will make the world a better place somehow? Huh ... " River was mentally testing this theory. A moment later, confusion writ all over his face, he said, "I don't see how you justify life by that when you are on a mission to die by default. Stifling your unique perspective is as good as not being present to your experience. Trading that for a mere concept of goodness ... it's disingenuous." He said the word slowly like it had taken a lot of practice to learn it.

River had a counter question, which was usually his best answer. "If you could be great, at the cost of being happy, would you choose it still? And would that be a valid choice—the better choice even?"

I had been over this in my head, "Maybe all the great people to have ever lived *did*. And that's probably how they earned their happiness."

What a cruel joke existence seemed to be to have played into. Jaya, my career, the life I planned with Rithvik—all of it was the life that I had built for myself. So now, just because I was feeling like rethinking it, I should give all of it up, deeming it to be divinely ordained?

That was how disposable my plans should be to honour innate volatile desires. That was self-love? That was prayer? Either that or one stays miserable within oneself.

"It is," I said, "The divine blackmail: 'Keep Flowing, or else ..."

River sighed. The divine blackmail: 'Keep Flowing, or else ... "So after everything, you're finally giving in to that black hole in the end—allowing it to consume you and deciding that to be the better existence."

The black hole. The tear in my fabric of existence. The disconnect. I mull this over now, and his question repeats in my head—'If you could be great at the cost of being happy, would you still choose it? And would that be a valid choice—the better choice even?' Before I could process the thought, River went on, "It's funny, jumpers always go in thinking the conflict is between what lays ahead of them or behind—the fear of the height in front or the safety of the ground behind them—when in fact, it is about the will of the person straddling the middle. Do they let the outside get in, or do they allow their insides to erupt outwards—that is the whole sport.

Oh, we ourselves are our greatest blind spot. We only register what we can see, perceive, and sense, and we can't do any of those with ourselves until we really look hard enough to see the most obvious. To see what we have grown most unseeing and numb to:

I can see you. I can't see me. I only know me, though—not you at all, not outside of my perception anyway, but do I trust that knowledge? Till I learn to, you keep filling me up, but I keep drowning myself out.

God ... was a smart cookie, after all. You had to learn of giving, I agree, but it had to go through you."

"What do you mean?"

"What I mean is ... isn't it odd that our imagery of God is, of all things, human?"

I frowned.

"By subjecting an infinite concept within our finite understanding, we also subject it to our own limitations: God comes with a gender, maybe parts of animals and birds. With human abilities, only exaggerated, like strength and healing. Maybe a few more gimmicky powers here and there. Those too, borrowed from what we see and wished as kids to have, like the ability to fly, skim the waters, hear what everyone is thinking, and some grown-up fantasies like turning water to wine."

Damn, is that true? I tried imagining a God that is actually beyond human and came up empty.

"You know why that is? Because we, as humans, are incapable of actual originality. There's nothing original we can really create. Did you know that you can't dream of anyone, not even a bystander, that you haven't seen somewhere in real life?

"The most original art we can create is, at best, an imitation of nature—but translated in our own unique way of processing it. You can only write of what is felt—and not a word more. We can only see as far as we have ever seen. You would have to feel kindness to truly give it. You would have to honour how life moulded you to solidify your relationship with it.

"Then, maybe, it is that chemistry that is unique, your interaction with the world—how it flows through you, and how it changes as it does, how *you* change as it does.

"As we've seen with the evolution of all other relationships, snuffing out individuality for the mirage of the relationship is compromising it by default. Puppeteering corpses doesn't make it a dance. Caging the storm within only suffocates the life out, and without your life, how can there be any experience of it?

"And oh, just like in any relationship, we really need to stop making an example out of one's selflessness and suffering, and congratulate their peace instead. That would be a far more loving thing to do, no? But I guess when you don't even know what contentment looks like and what it makes people capable of, how would you know your system is actually a failure, right? I don't see how any relationship would be any different. Whether it is the one you share with a partner, your work, or the society it serves. Or even God."

It was getting late, and I gestured for the cheque. The evening was coming to a close. River sat still. "Maybe the edge must not be the place for you. It exaggerates everything—the fears, the will, the courage—the *you*, and turns one inside out. It is not the place one goes to die but where one goes to remember how to live! To be *alive.* To engage in a dialogue between all of you and all of life."

"Yes, yes, a LIVER. I remember ... " and after a silent moment of thought, I added, "And I've already qualified, so no going back on your word."

We pay and get up. River looked me straight in the eye and said, "So show me if you're ready. Show me the most version of you and show me if you can at least *see* it without panicking and without anxiety, because if you aren't ready—well, maybe, you aren't ready."

Whoa, for a liver, he was dead serious. "Fine then. Don't judge me when I do."

"Don't judge *you* when you do."

We walked out soon after, and the cold consumed us all at once. He rode away on his motorbike into the night, and I made my way back to my cosy little tent. As I walked away from the circus of lights around the Ganga, it grew pitch dark. I knew only of the rustling of the grass below my feet and the cicadas that grew louder with every step, humming quite madly like children on a sugar high. A couple of minutes later, there at a distance, it stood, looming closer. The light from my tent grew bigger, and I ran into its warmth. A long night lay ahead of me.

Chapter 24

I was nowhere close to sleep. As soon as I had stepped back into my tent, I unwrapped my stole, whipped out my notepad, and got straight to it. I would have to write my thoughts all over again, but this story seemed simpler. All it demanded was to unleash myself, which was probably the easiest thing to do and the hardest thing to start upon. How could something as simple as that be the answer? Stop. This time, I'm determined. No more double-guessing myself. No more mind chatter. Having unlocked the identity I had been strangling down in chains, my thoughts come, one spilling over the other, just like the coffee I hastily brew.

It was a fairly simple solution, really. Stupidly simple.

I looked at my bullet points for the hundredth time: Manpower, money, stability, visible misery, sustainability. If I'm being honest with myself, as a brand strategist working on a pro bono project for Dharma Foundation, outside of this warped pandemic timeline, my first obvious objectives would be to boost its visibility, build credibility and enhance its trust within its target market—a crucial currency for an NGO surviving primarily on voluntary donations. It would still not cater to the most important flaw in the plan: at least enough stability to ensure sustenance. For a stable flow of human resources, so far in the form of erratic volunteers, they would need employees. For a stable flow of money, they would need income. I pause. Now that it was on paper, I really couldn't see any other solution.

What social service needed was business.

For this, I would need to go beyond marketing and design—a modification for the product itself. There was only one other time I had ever done this. The beverage and a pinch of turmeric. It was the only time I had ever dared to let the story of the brand dictate the product—and how it had worked. I feel the remnants of that shame start to creep back up again.

No. I won't allow it. This time, I'm determined to power through, not lifting my eyes from the notepad.

The task at hand would entail:

- A study of their key skills—since they didn't have a single-pointed forte, this would be hard, but it also allowed me the liberty to choose from the variety of services they rendered. These had to be such that they could be leveraged financially. Since they had most notably worked on emergency relief, their skills would presumably include SOS organisation, first-aid training, and panic relief. This was enough to build on.
- Then, there was a rudimentary interest audit, which was simply talking to the team about what they would be most passionate about pursuing. Almost always overlooked, this was as key to sustainability as the

availability of tangible resources. What they did was usually a result of their means, but how *well* they did it—that depended on how much they liked doing it. The heart of it all was always the epicentre of its actions.

- Then, Market Research, a study of those most likely to purchase from them and then curating the product to suit their needs. This was the oldest marketing practice in the world—observing what the demand is for in the market and creating its supply. It was just creating a solution for the problems their beneficiaries face.

I stared at it. The crudely scribbled plan led to something. Towards furthering my ideation, I was missing a crucial element: feedback from the customer.

I video called River. There was literally nobody else I was left with. The thought pinched before I brushed it aside. Not now.

This was the first video call I made to him because I knew from our more elaborate R&D (Research and Development) drives that feedback came from more than verbal cues. It came from what they responded to and how they absorbed information.

He picked up on the sixth ring. I knew because I was impatiently counting.

"This is new," he started, his face bemused.

"Hello to you too! You asked me to show you the *most* version of me. This is it. This is what I would do now, what I *may* do.... if it makes sense. Tell me?"

"You're crazy, you know that?" River said with a smile and a frown simultaneously sprouting up on his face.

"Yes, I've been told that a lot lately, and that's beside the point," I had nowhere else to be and yet blurted the plan out in a rush.

After I did, I felt the need to add, "Of course, this is all just based on an informal initial chat with Mr Kharbanda. This would be built upon… But I reckon something like an institution of online training on crisis management would work well. They used to run a school—that had started it all, except that these would be paid. It is a much-needed service, sold for its value by people who had field experience to share.

"So short-term workshops, maybe a series on life skills like how to stay calm during panic situations, where they share personal experiences, teach basic first-aid, even sustenance-rationed cooking, evacuation procedures and such…should have a good market. Especially now, when this generation has just witnessed a crisis and realised first-hand how inadequately we are all prepared for it. It could be something like 'The Art of War' after that book…or like a 'Train for a rainy day' with an umbrella logo…" I had been brainstorming out loud when I looked up. River hadn't said a word so far. He had the same blank expression he did when he had torn himself away from his book back at the café.

He adjusted his face and cleared his throat.

"Well?" I egg him on. If I came here looking for feedback, he was giving me none.

"Your eyes light up when you talk through your work. It's like watching an artist play with their colours. Why would you ever want to lose that?"

Why would I want to lose that? I remember my conflict, and now that some steam had been blown off, I buckled under the answer. I flap my notepad shut. Creative though it was, it had been an entirely futile exercise.

"Because. It takes away from the essence of what they stand for: *Service for service's sake.* To give what one can. Adding money to the mix is to divert their objective to profits, invite stakeholders who are in it for other reasons, like employees who are part of the initiative for the job instead of the intention and build a business on others' fears.

"Traditionally, religiously, or spiritually speaking, it feels like *sacrilege...* You don't look for returns from what you give, let alone gains. That makes it selfish, doesn't it? Shouldn't there be some things that are selfless? And to answer your question, it's not about what lights up my eyes. I'm trying my hardest to be what lights up the room ... you know?"

River stayed silent a whole minute, his expression unreadable. Then, very matter-of-factly, he says, "You mentioned something about that at Chai Library. Let's get into it then. So you think that God thinks that losing yourself will make you more useful to the world?"

It wasn't a patronising question but a genuine one. I knew that about him by now and liked that the most about River. This allowed for full conversations on incomplete thoughts. Not necessarily the destination but the journey. Which eventually was most progressive in actually arriving there.

"The beauty of renunciation? Here's hoping that that may finally be what makes me a better person. It's not that it's not annoying. I just think it's what it is. I think maybe we become ... full only to realise it isn't nearly enough. Eventually leading us to let go of our delusions. Maybe it is only in selflessness that we find meaning for ourselves. It is mostly vain though. That's why I said it. That if I were God, I'd design it differently—because if we are just to receive the world and let it flow through us, as it may, without any obstruction, what do *we* exist for?

"What, then, is the purpose of our being? To whip up dreams, only to let them go in the end? If observing and appreciating is all we're here to do; of what *is*, then what is the point of ever imagining or creating what can be? Aren't we supposed to be active participants in our world?"

On this metaphoric bridge I was treading on, every time I thought I was making progress, there was that inexplicable pull backwards and this tug of war felt rather like being caught in a loop.

River started slowly, "What if God turns out to be the sum of all things? A God that is dependent on the harmony and well-oiled functioning among all that exists, as you exist within an elaborately designed body—nowhere inside it, and yet permeating through all of it: the blood, the skin, the bones."

I realise that it is a wondrous thing to witness someone's faith. I am taken aback by its sheer weight. Fluid but fierce, it was just like River.

I go completely quiet and look down at my plan.

"But what about doing things from love? It is only normal to want to be selfless from love?"

River said, "Ah, love. Oh, I'd hate to think there is a 'normal' definition of it somewhere because 'normal' is just another prejudice. The most all-encompassing one at that. Once we establish an idea as 'normal', we see everything different from it as 'deviant', and that replaces our curiosity with judgment.

"Normal love can also look like ... self-*full*, no?

"If you ever get to witness that, you realise very quickly that 'self-lessness' is such a paltry insult to love. Love is always *more*. That's why it is so special. If you've ever loved anyone or anything wholly, you'll know that it could never diminish you. Far from it, in fact, it leaves you enriched from your act of loving, and you are never 'lesser' for it.

"That's what makes it magical, isn't it? How the rules of transactions don't apply. How you, the giver, can be quenched by the watering itself, allowing you the privilege of making the bloom a part of you. So then, what is love but extending your *life* to something outside of it? Expanding beyond the self, enough to include its buoyance within your own river.

"Love isn't what leaves you parched. It is how you become an ocean. How can that ever be selfless?—it is *wholesome*. Karma ... must work the same way. It's ironic how people talk about selflessness and, in the next breath, how it would earn them good karma. That's the hook. How many would do good if they knew for sure it wasn't coming back to them? Goodness is and has always been murky business. But one doesn't usurp karma points individually like it's a loyalty program in a retail store with a rainbow of happiness at the end. One allows it to happen through us for the whole to up its game. The goodness itself is the gift, and the world is richer for it. Just because you created it doesn't make it any less of a gift.

"I'd rather be imperfect in my authenticity than be perfect in another's plan. It is an act of my faith—I do it as an offering of my prayer.

"Seeing sustainability as selfish is like reducing your purpose—and the love that drives it—into a ... depreciating asset.

"It must become about 'all of me' building something wholesome with *all* of life. How do I create something unique out of that—now, *that* would be a beautiful conversation to have."

I always marvel at just how much strength people draw from something as tender as love.

"How exactly would you know the difference between this and that?"

River gave out a boyish laugh.

"By what you look for and what you see. It isn't righteousness that determines the quality of a relationship. It is *connection*. That is your tether to them. Without that, it's only ever going to be a liability.

"If it's causing you to lessen yourself, it's the wrong direction for your love. Arbitrary rules, without consideration of the individual experience, can only ever assert a transaction, not a relationship. Because can you really *be* connected to something you don't reveal yourself to?

"So become you, the most you, with a determined detachment to anything that hinders that journey. That's all you're supposed to do. That is how Godliness flows through you."

I stared blankly at the screen and said, "Self-love, River? That's your answer to an existential crisis? Really?" I laughed.

River smiled sheepishly. "Not when you say it like that. But surely, you would rather have the verb of lovingness than the idea of it?" He winked, then added as an afterthought, "Besides, commanding one's value can never decrease it. Sounds like if you don't, you may be able to spare a couple of hours a month sacrificially. If you do, you allow it to earn your years. Sounds pretty obvious to me, but hey, this is just my opinion..."

I'm kind of shocked at the dots that he was connecting in front of me like a magician.

It's funny how we make rooms out of vastness and imagine holding the key to one and a lock to another—when it is only our illusion of a barrier that prohibits entry.

It is also the mind that always had access to any room, for there never were any.

So it was self-love, but it was more. It was a connection, our sense of belonging, that determined the quality of our contentment. That's the eternal struggle, the great fight, and the final difference between an average life and a great one. Finding that connection with what we allow to consume us. Even with all the complexities of modernisation, we really are no different from the misfit weed that continues to fight for ground till the day it wilts. And for a connection to work, its pieces have to fit right. Simply, just right, and that's what makes it perfect. Therefore, self-knowledge. It isn't the big picture that solves the puzzle. It is observing the structure of the pieces that make it. That is how it can be drawn out of them, although that is neither the objective nor the route. The larger picture is only the illusion that holds the process—keeps the cogs turning—and that is probably its only purpose. River was right, wasn't he? May we never reduce our love to an unfortunate depreciating asset. May it be fed enough to become fuel. To thrive so as to nourish.

I sat, clutching my phone and my papers, processing. Building friendships, making money, creating contentment, understanding philosophy and morality, marketing and innovation and service, finding a purpose, deepening devotion and through it all, weaving the stories we tell ourselves that tie them all together—everything that makes a life well *lived*...

It's actually pretty brilliant how it all boils down to the art of relationships—and how the only real way of accessing that knowledge is through unveiling the artistry within oneself.

"So ... ?" I looked down at my notes. "Did I have something here?"

"I think you just might. Don't discard you. Use you. For that, you must find *you*. You seem to know where to look. Don't stop now."

Not stopping now, I repeat to myself in declaration. Towards that end, I added, "Oh and by the way, on the subject of God, we have been limiting too. We can only see as far as we have ever seen. Why else would we call God a 'He'?"

There. Aligning with my beliefs now.

He looked up, knowing the night was coming to a close and inhaled deeply. "Let's change that, shall we? Here on out, God will forever be they/them."

River ended with a flourish, "And just like that, we're another step closer to understanding 'them' by letting our delusions—a past knowledge fall away ... "

I yawn. "Goodnight, River."

"Night, Nanki."

I clicked off, finally allowing the night to take me under.

Wholesome, I think.

It had been a wholesome evening indeed.

I woke up knowing what I had to do that day. Maybe it was the restful sleep or the soulful conversations. Or maybe it was because I now actually had the skeleton of a plan.

Whatever it was, I knew that I hadn't quite seen the whole picture yet, only the past. A lot of answers about the future—those would come from the present.

Mr Kharbanda's *son*. He wasn't involved in the organisation—or was he? And why not? What was his vision for its future?

There was only one way I could find out: This meant I had to go rafting.

Oh, what adventures was Rishikesh going to bring me?

Chapter 25

I stood under the scorching sun by eleven a.m. that morning, all set with my sports shoes and my hair tied back in a swishy ponytail. Not that I had to walk any distance, but I felt the need to armour my body. I had loved rafting as a child, but things have a way of seeming like a joyride when you're squished between your parents with the luxury of leaving your fears to them. Alone, now that's a whole different story. There was no one to extricate my body out of this terrifying, chaotic Ganga should it be needed.

I approach the gushing river, dancing to a rhythm only she knew the notes to, in ripples all her own. As I trudged over the round pebbles adorning the riverbed, a man turned around, and I swear I could've identified him anywhere despite never having met him: Mr Kharbanda's son carried forth his stature and his face, minus a couple of decades. He waved out to me.

"Nanki! Hello there. I'm Karan." No handshakes for social distancing.

I reciprocate and smile. "Hey Karan! Finally we meet. I'm so excited about this!" and looking out at the rapids, I bite my lip and add, "I think."

He gives out a laugh that I can tell will age just like his father's and says, "It's okay if you're scared. You will be more certain once we're in there. So shall we chat over the raft, then?" It was a hypothetical question, and he had already started turning towards the black raft tethered to the pier.

Oh God, here we go.

"We will have another couple on the raft. We are taking a minimal number of people for social distancing. Please sanitise your hands before and after, and keep your mask on where possible. Ah—here's your life jacket. Strap it on—this will be a 16-km-long route. We are now at Shiv Puri and will raft down to main Rishikesh within three hours. There are Grade II and Grade III rapids en route, which denotes their difficulty level. This means it is a moderate route but includes a couple of major rapids, like the 'Double Trouble' and the 'Return to Sender' ... "

Excuse me? Did he just say, 'Return to sender?'—What the hell had I signed up for? I strap myself into my lifejacket, look up at the vast blue sky, sigh, and go in. The water swirled and gushed around me. She was happy—the Ganga. Ecstatic, actually.

Wild and free.

I skimmed my fingers through its freezing waters, forming a trail of an adoring caress, leaving an imprint of my love for just a moment before the river consumed it whole and flowed eternally on. The raft swayed.

Karan had been briefing the couple so far, who, by the looks of them, were on their honeymoon.

The woman wore the traditional red bangles and was heavily made up, while her husband, also smartly dressed, had his hands firmly glued to hers. It must have been half an hour by the time he carefully scuttled back and settled opposite me.

"All good so far? We have a rapid coming up in a bit. We'll have to row then."

"All great!" I say, sitting tighter now, awaiting the storm. "Thanks for arranging this on such short notice!"

"Ah, my pleasure...T'was the least I could do! Besides, isn't the weather just perfect today?

"Absolutely stunning," I say mindlessly and rush forth before I lose my chance. "So when I met your dad—phenomenal work, by the way. We are so beyond indebted ... "

Some things put into everyday words sound so regular when they are anything but.

The couple looked over. I mouth a rough 'Hi' and explained, "You guys must've read about Dharma Foundation during lockdown?"

The woman looked to the husband mutely, and the husband nodded vaguely, like I was speaking a different language.

"No? Oh, okay, they were distributing oxygen cylinders to people's homes for those that couldn't get a hospital bed ... "

"Ah, yes, I think I saw their name on Instagram. Yes, I think I remember now," he looked confused about why I would bring that up, and I explained, gesturing towards Karan, "It's theirs! His father started the organisation."

I said it like I was introducing a superstar. He responded like I was a child showing off a new toy. The man looked towards him appreciatively and said, "Wow, that's great, bud. Good initiative!" Karan beamed, partly amused.

Great initiative? That's it? No one close to him went through the horror of Viral-X, did they? It hadn't touched him personally just yet. Well, I sighed. Good for him. It was easy to tell such people apart now. That's a weird kind of superpower to have earned after one had made it across that bridge. His wife nudged him just then to take pictures of the scene in front, and he diligently whipped out his phone and posed, as if on cue, for a series of clearly well-practised selfies. Pouting and all.

New love makes people stupid, I declared to myself and turned back to Karan. He was grinning sheepishly.

"Well, I wouldn't have understood it till I saw it either. And maybe not even then. It's taken me this long to understand why I needed to hunt down the source of this light."

He sat there, smiling quietly. The mountains did too. The river cajoled the rest of the words out. "It was a dark time, wasn't it? Oof, I was dunked so far deep into darkness that a little sliver of light, and I couldn't see anything else. It almost forces you to wonder what it would be like to come up for air, to get close to this hope, to be soaked in it… to become it."

Had it been any other time, she probably never would have cut this deep. But everyone seemed connected now—bonded by the same grief, the same fears, the same trials of the same time. The married couple seemed exempt from it somehow, which was okay too. I looked at them, blissfully unconcerned with anything outside of themselves, and smiled.

"I honestly just came here chasing butterflies—"

"I don't think so, Ma'am," he interrupted me for the first time. He had been looking at me keenly so far, and his voice was kind. "I think you came here chasing hope. That isn't an entirely futile pursuit of life. It is probably the bravest." He smiled warmly with an understanding that I felt grateful for.

Nothing binds people together more than shared pain. Mr Kharbanda's voice echoed in my ears.

"In that case, is it okay if I pick your brain over this after?"

"Definitely, you can! I'm afraid I may not have much to say, though. I managed to give very little time to it. But wait back after and we'll chat?"

I nodded.

He held up his hand to stop me from going on. "Brace yourself. We have a Rollercoaster coming up."

He jumped up and announced the rapids on the horizon. They had been instructed on how to row in the beginning, and the atmosphere was suddenly charged.

This, here. Moments that demand you to crawl out of your head make for better plans. The conversation can wait. This moment and this wave will not. I looked at the ominous rapid coming up. That tingling in my toes that churn in my stomach—excitement. Yes, I knew it with certainty now: I really was excited.

I held on tight.

Karan gave out a war cry: "Let's start rowing backwards. Full force, everyone! Let's welcome Rollercoaster! Har Har Gange!"

Everyone joined the chorus: "*Har Har Gange*!!!" I started to row backwards. The husband stood up for a video and had to be sat down to balance the float. All too suddenly, the waters turned turbulent, and there was an uproar of waves fiercely rushing into each other. The raft swayed dangerously, managing to stay above it all only by the edge of its teeth. As we danced above the waves, rowing with all the force we could muster, the frigid water splashed into the raft, and everyone in it looked at each other, now drenched—and giggled. Once past it, the raft calmed down and resumed a peaceful flow down the stream, only until the next one came along.

Karan operated out of a small office. I sat across from his desk while he stepped out to get me a cutting chai from the stall next door. I looked around me—plastered with posters of rafting, the pale blue walls barely peeked through.

I was drenched but couldn't care less.

Rithvik. I wanted to share it with him. Yell it out, in fact. I typed out the message: Guess who just went rafting!! Wish you were here! It was INCREDIBLE....

I almost sent it. Almost. I sighed. All these yells and nowhere to go. Instead, I write in notes to myself:

The habit is the ghost,
Dead,
but only almost.

Yep, I'm officially talking to myself now.

"Here we are!" Karan walked in with two tiny, serrated glasses of tea and placed one in front of me.

"Ah," is all I could manage as I hold the glass close. Its scalding heat made me extremely conscious of how cold and wet I was. He sat down and, rubbing his hands together, started, "Yes, so. How can I help you?"

I'm extremely aware of how noisily I sip through my teeth, "Thanks for this! I've been a demanding guest, and your family has been the most kind."

Karan answered playfully, "Just what we do. We're in the business of being kind."

"About that. Just wanted your take on things, actually. I think initially, I was curious about the scope of work, either like you—or through you. Like I said earlier, I was just sort of inspired to a blinding degree, I guess. In comparison to what you guys were doing, everything else seemed to have washed out.

"But I didn't know where to start, and that's when I met Mr Kharbanda. I was wondering what kind of contribution you would most benefit from, what was the most needed. He said you are flooded with funds and volunteers presently—though I'm sure more are welcome.

"Something he said about sustainability made me think of some sustainable solutions, though. I was just not sure if you would be open to looking at regular income streams and running a commercial wing as a parallel unit to your volunteering work."

As I said it, it sounded comical. Who wouldn't want regular income streams? I also simultaneously felt he might judge me for degrading their purpose. Vilifying it, cheapening it. Implying their stupidity almost. As if they couldn't have done that themselves if they had wanted it.

"Of course, we would—it depends on how." He sat ahead with his fingers locked in front of him. Again, just like his father.

"Oh!" I exclaimed, relief washing over me. "I was worried. I wanted to respect that you chose not to ... "

Karan put down his glass of cutting chai.

"You think we chose this? Nanki, the intention was—and is—definitely to serve, but when that service demands resources, and you find most of yours being spent on sourcing those resources—effort and energy that should be spent on the service you set out to extend, it soon starts feeling more like a liability.

"But we didn't know how to restructure because, by the time we realised it, our heart was already invested in this living, breathing baby of ours, this beautiful brainchild with all the potential in the world. Before it can reach that potential, though, it breaks down and needs to be built up again. It's honestly heartbreaking. But we didn't want to let the people down. Some of them have supported us BECAUSE we're not commercial. Over time, as I saw it, it became like a toxic relationship that I didn't want my life to become about."

The words immediately took me back to my chat with River, and I nodded knowingly.

Karan went on, "And let me tell you something I've realised. We were also commercial—you have to be to exist in the market. We had to sell misery. Not just throw the spotlight on facts but actually emotionalise it, dress up the grief and sell it. It wouldn't sell otherwise. Earning charity is its own kind of business. I don't think it was seen that way. But that's what you have to do, to inspire donations to scale up. When you're out in the field, you realise there's so much more work to be accomplished. You can't feed nine kids on the street and let the tenth go hungry, watching everyone else get fed. It creates desperation. To the end customer, all it translates to is a spam call. I'd rather do good work and command its value. But we weren't businessmen. We don't understand this—not well enough to compete anyway."

It's funny. I remembered feeling exactly that way when I looked at that man in his PPE kit that morning from my terrace. What could I possibly do? What value could I possibly bring to the table?

"My father was a government servant and is now living on his pension after retirement. Why do you think I didn't do that full-time and took up this job? I am so proud of the work we do, but dreams need fuel. In an ideal world, they wouldn't, but in an ideal world, we also wouldn't need to mend grief. So if we're in the game, whether we like it or not, we might as well learn the rules—that's the only way we can ace them."

Something River had said a while back came back to me now: 'When goodness succeeds, goodness thrives.' I can honestly appreciate the gravity of that thought only today. Goodness will always be enough, but for it to be the absolute rule, the law of the land, it must also win. 'We really need to stop making an example out of one's selflessness and suffering, and congratulate their peace instead. That would be a far more loving thing to do, no?' Yes, I think now. As I sit looking at Karan, I see before me how that plays out and the consequences of not heeding it.

We need to stop lauding selflessness, I thought fiercely. Not because it isn't noble but because it is unfortunate and glorifying it keeps the doer in more of it. It ties their identity to it, and even at best, even if from love, they only know to stay in and gift this suffrage forward because they were only ever celebrated for that: their failure and exhaustion and drainage. It is only when people come from a long line of suffocation, I realised, to cope, they attach virtue to suffering and honour to pain. The children, who have not known of the pain, just of this learning, internalise it and perpetuate it: with honour, they associate pain; with virtue, they equate repression.

Until someone finally decides that feasting on crumbs doesn't make a hearty meal. Like Karan. In their little acts of self-love, they revolutionise the act of loving itself, and it forever stands changed. Having seen the cause and now the consequence of the Dharma Foundation, it finally made sense and clicked into place: At some point, we have to have the courage to own our pain and call it wrong. That is how we begin.

"Okay then," I said. "I may have a plan."

Chapter 26

It seemed to have become a hybrid. That's what it was. As far as I knew, it didn't have a label exactly—it was just the strengths of two different worlds fusing together to form a new thing. I smile as I think over this now with my eyes shut as we sit in yet another meditation session. It had been two weeks since that meeting with Karan, and we had been building this new wing for Dharma, page by page, idea upon idea. This was a much smaller scale than the projects I was used to. After some rudimentary planning and exciting brainstorming sessions, we had launched 'Kurukshetra', meaning the sacred battlefield—a training institution to cultivate the spirit of a warrior prepared for combat. 'The Art of War' was the tagline. Mr Kharbanda had loved that one. I had it incorporated into their website within three days of basic artwork direction and execution. By the seventh day, we had rolled it out on social media after planning schedules for online training workshops with the employees and volunteers. During the organisation of such logistics, while having to understand their portfolio of work, I was stunned at the experience they had accumulated. They had so much knowledge, they just didn't know how to commercialise it.

But I understand its value and have an idea of its positioning in the market. This is where—and now I could think of it with pride—I shine.

River had been right. As I started feeling this fullness in myself, I could see the value I bring and the route it could take through me. *We are how we access the world,* I thought. The cool Himalayan breeze hugged me, and I came to see what my purpose had been. To bring myself to the table was all that was required because nobody had ever charted the exact same route or witnessed my unique landmarks. It wasn't this or that. It was *everything.* What had to be charted was simply the 'how'. All my questions had been valid; all my experiences led me *here*. The past hadn't been a waste, after all. Not the good, not the bad, not the ugly. Not even the shame from that turmeric tip; it was how I had the confidence to do this today. It didn't happen to me. It had happened *for* me. To make me uniquely perfect for my imagination from here.

A pinch of turmeric, I thought. That meeting came back to me now, and for the first time, I didn't feel the need to dig deeper within myself from shame. It was over. Just like that, what had taken hold since that day finally let go of me, and I realised how light it can feel to be free.

The road always forks into two …

Had I not had the courage to take one step ahead of another, even when I couldn't see the way, I would've been heavy with unfortunate luggage for the rest of my years. But because I did, my obstacles became opportunities—just stepping stones on my path. Poison turned to medicine, just like that, with a mere shift of perspective, and we say—we don't have magic. As I inhale, I feel it dawn on me. Creating this life, this connection with feeling alive—it is divinity, it's God, it is magic. To become disconnected from it is to be disconnected from it all. And without it all, what do we even have?

The fear is whether life will still love you back when you do.

Vulnerability, then, is the final key. The strength it takes to be fragile enough to *be* and to allow being seen and to build from there. A silent promise to uphold the consequences that flow through us, for that is how the connection with life is honoured and strengthened. That's the most important one of all. I was probably failing meditation again today, but it was more than okay. Today marks one week after launching Kurukshetra, and it has been garnering such a buzz! Since Dharma had been attracting media anyway for their brilliant ongoing work amidst the pandemic, this too has started getting noticed by the press.

As I grew stronger, I knew down to my bones that only I could have made this as robust as it was.

My phone buzzes. I can hear Pihu huff, but my eyes fly open to see a text from Mr Kharbanda.

"First milestone achieved. On day 7 of launch, we have officially made bookings worth Rupees One Lakh by hitting our thirty-fourth customer. Thank you bete! Transferring Rupees Ten Thousand to you for your service. Please accept this as a token of our appreciation. You must do more of this work. You are very good at it."

Oh, sweet lord, he had sent me money! I think I might cry. I feel like I've been handed a report emblazoned with an A+.

It was in this moment that I feel it for the first time. I was going to be just fine in the world.

It was a windy day, and Pihu got out a stack of papers from her mandala-art-adorned duffel bag. The class had been a good one today, and I felt this knowing that my time with these meditation sessions amidst these glorious mountains and these pristine beams of sunlight was almost up.

One just knows that sort of stuff, don't they? Want it or not, you can feel an experience start to peel away from your life, like wallpaper that's lived its time. Deny it as much as you want, and add all the adhesive you need; when it's done, it's just... done.

Pihu had an unreadable expression on her face as she started to hand out leaflets to the five members of the class today.

A blank white page with this written in bold:

#IftheWorldCrashesDown.
Not a goodbye.

I looked up for an explanation. Was it just me, or was something off about her today?

"This is an initiative by a local Viral-X hospital here. As we all know, the Kumbh Mela is almost upon us. The number of cases has already been increasing, our hospitals are already full to capacity, and after this... " She fidgeted nervously and paced herself. What was that look in her eyes? Was it fear?

"Well, after this, we don't know what's coming for us. As you all make your way back to your homes before the storm hits, here is what we hope for." She held up a leaflet.

"Find a piece of Rishikesh that means something to you. Make it your own. Write words of love on it and carry them back safely. Identify the people who've meant something to you in this life and let them know. Send this to them and send it far and wide.

"Let the language be yours and its expression. Let the words be yours and what you write them on—a pebble from the Ganga, a leaf from a tree, or a tissue paper from your favourite cafe.

"Tell them what they mean to you if the world crashes down. Tell them this is not a goodbye. This is just—" her voice cracked. "Rishikesh's love letter to the world."

I looked down at my leaflet. Oh, this was morbid.

"You can leave. Come with me!" I feel the urgency to save her.

"And go where? This is home," She smiled through her eyes welling up.

That moment right there, blue hair fluttering in the wind, eyes blazing, prepared to go down with the ship—that was how I would always remember her.

Pihu touched my hand warmly, sniffled away the overwhelm and said determinedly, "Don't worry about me. This is not about the fear—it is of courage."

...And I will never, ever forget that.

Yes, time's almost up. One day to Bungy.

I guess Rishikesh wasn't done with me yet because I still had this last thing to do: a couple of love letters to find.

Chapter 27

The most tender of them all, and yet, this is my toughest task so far. I stroll down to Ram Jhula today in search of my canvas. Pieces of Rishikesh to stow away. I had already collected a couple of items—A pebble from the bed of the Ganges. Even if it was stolen away from the riverbed, it will always have the river to thank for its smoothened roundedness. This was for Jaya. A tissue from Chai Library—this one was for me. When I went to get it, I had scribbled on it:

'A reminder that life is too short for 'fine,' and to never settle for anything less than spectacular. Oh, and also, that if only you bring yourself to a great cup of chai, you will always manage to find the company to go with it.

Just as long as you bring yourself to the table.

With Love, The version of me, from Rishikesh.'

I had three more to find. In all of my thirty-three—almost thirty-four years now, I had only five love letters to give. And one of those was to myself. *Oh, well.*

I walk along the market with rows of little stores crammed next to each other, selling handicrafts, cheap clothes, jute handbags, strings of Rudraksha beads, dream catchers, and so much more than my eyes could absorb. I am looking for a very specific thing, though. I wonder if it would still even be here. As a child, my parents and I would religiously come here for it. A rare fruit, the shape of a scarlet teardrop: The Ram-Phal. Literally translating to the fruit of Lord Ram, it was named after this area because it was only available here. I remember thinking that it must be a magical creation of Rishikesh's soil, a tangible realisation of all its myths. Now, I wonder how that was even possible, but come to think of it, I had never spotted that fruit anywhere else. I walked down to the end of the street, right up to the Ram Jhula footbridge—and there it was. A woman squatted with a basket bursting with that beautiful Ram-Phal, split in two, bleeding a red I had only ever seen this fruit to have.

I go up to her and ask for a couple to be bagged and one for now. With a toothy grin and plastic gloves, she cut a fresh one up, salted it with *anardana* masala and handed it to me on a leaf as a plate. Within its fleshy shell, it held juicy red pearls, almost like a pomegranate's. I bite into it eagerly. Tangy, mildly sweet with a delicious sourness! Oh, it was just as I remembered it. I'm surprised at how well I remembered it, in fact. All of it came back—the laughter, the togetherness, the love. It's amazing how tastes, smells, and places can become keys for a whole bank of memories. At that moment, I realised it was always a choice: Happiness. I could choose what to do with this access now. I can yearn for what was, or I can be grateful for what I've had. Everything is going to be a passing station in this journey anyway.

Then I found my third love letter.

The large fig tree with unusually dangly roots that is right behind the grinning lady selling *Ram-Phal*. I pluck a leaf, a big broad leaf off of it—a symbol of that epiphany—and that was that!

On my way back, I had also found a fourth love letter, but first things first.

I opened my mail for the first time since I had come here. I let the barrage of emails flood in. I wasn't attending to them right now. I signed the pebble with the hashtag: '#IftheWorldCrashesDown. Not a goodbye.' I click a photo of it, attach the image to the email and write:

'Dear ~~Jaya~~ Work Mom,

So your work-child is a teenager now. I can only imagine the horror.

Please accept this as my resignation. Your child is only moving out, not moving on. You don't move on from family. Thank you for never giving up on me.

You're right: I do owe you answers. I was only waiting to find them. Please find attached the business plan for my new journey. It has all the details of the project I've been working on and its returns so far. It wasn't a project when I started it, but it has shown me new potential—and faith is nothing if not a bet on potential. You taught me that by example. So, I'm daring to have faith now.

In a gist, I intend to reach out to add a sustainable income stream to organisations working on charities or donations, market a new commercial line, rebrand and sell for people who need the know-how. Basically, what I was doing for the fizzy drink, just for people who need it more. For people needed more. Those doing the work, the world would be richer for. I can handle the project for six months till they take off and charge a ten percent off the profits earned during that time. The details can be worked out. How I've struggled with the service and payment bit. It isn't a service till I've suffered—seemed to have been an operative subconscious thought. Maybe it was survivors' guilt.

I've had to rewire myself and question my beliefs around work, money, and how it all ties with the idea of self and community and service. While I was walking a path of self-immolation, what I came upon instead was kind of like a crash course on Money EQ—our emotional intelligence around currency.

I've come to realise that 'selflessness' can be wholesome as long as the intention is detached from its reward but cultivated as fuel by disciplined work. In my proposal, the progress of the work is tracked from impact, not profit, but the impact demands profit, which is not going to remain a blind spot—it will be seen and attended to with the spirit of service. An empowering one, if you will.

I am also attaching a picture of a souvenir I'm carrying back for you.

Until then, stay safe.

With Love,

from Rishikesh.'

A whoosh and sent.

I brewed myself a cup of coffee. I had two more letters of love to get through.

I wanted to finish the book I had started on my first day here and had a last couple of pages left. I carried it along with my mug to relish by the Ganges.

I made my way down the familiar path, taking in the crunch of the grass, the view of the mountains, and the pure air.

I sat by the roaring river, my feet dunked in its now not-so-freezing water. I spend a couple of hours watching the sun, waves, and people pass me by as I read.

Then, without warning, my phone buzzes with the notification of an incoming mail.

I sit up straight. It was Jaya.

Dear Nanki,

It pains me to see you leave. I believed so very much in the dreams I saw for you.

But it is not my place to dream for you. So, let's crack a deal. One last time.

Don't expect me to be entirely happy about this, and I wouldn't expect you to change your life decisions based on that. Deal?

In its own way, this loss is its own victory. Because now I know I've raised you better than to be satisfied with being a people pleaser. You're a lot like Nanu, but you're also a little like me.

This mad belief you have, this stubborn optimism about time being worth salvaging, life being more lived, the world standing a chance, and the will to chase your happiness: I held the very same faith when I stepped into the advertising world forty years back.

For me to forever think of you as my protégé, it was never the result or the road that I looked for to be the same: it was the spirit.

I did well.

Fly, my child. Consider this as my official acceptance of your resignation.

A social entrepreneur. That should be on your new visiting cards.

Yours,
Work Mom

My heart swelled with utter joy. Social entrepreneur! So there *was* a label for this. Trust Jaya to always know. Moms always know. I'd have to look into this and study it to deepen my understanding—but what else was all of my life for? I feel like I could dance!

I feel so ... free! A burden off my chest.

One of them anyway: it was time for the next letter of love.

I don't think pain is inflicted. I think you have it in you all along, and you seek out ways to feel it. This is why, for my parents, I know what I'm taking: this version of me from Rishikesh. Yes, I am becoming their letter of love. Possibly, my favourite piece of Rishikesh. They deserve that. People spend far too much time dissecting why they are the way they are and far too little on what to do about it. I won't let my insufferable mind implicate my parents—they were doing their best. What happened as collateral damage is my job to heal, not theirs. Maybe my finding of peace can finally release us all.

Maybe it's time to let them in. To let them all in.

Which brings me to my next.

On my way from Ram Jhula market, I picked up a CD of those trippy tantric songs that wafted through all the little streets of Rishikesh. No one used CDs anymore, but oh well, it was symbolic anyway.

I wanted to do this before I left, before my Bungy. When I walked down that yellow bridge from River's video, I wanted to know that I had truly made it through my warpath.

So this has to be done… and this has to be done now.

I open my chat window with Rithvik. It laid vacant like it had all of this month. He hadn't called once. I had to remind myself that I was the one to have asked for space.

Like an idiot, he gave it. Who does that?

Listen, endings don't mean having a personality transplant, but I've thought long and hard about this. I do think that someone like me actually needs someone like him to work with. Our individual flaws have the potential of cancelling each others' out. Maybe that's the best we get. Not a haloed individual free of toxicity, but rather someone whose demons dance well with ours. I pace the room. I centre myself with a quick five-minute meditation, inhaling and exhaling deeply to gather my thoughts, retracing back to my sense of *connection* with him, before I begin:

'If the world crashes down, this is my not-a-Goodbye.

Dear Rithvik,

Did I ever tell you of the exact moment I knew?

My family had already liked you from early on, from when our families would all meet socially. They would tease me about dating you for some reason, but I would brush them off. It was obviously not then.

Then, that one New Year's Eve, when we were all tenting out in that God-forsaken place, getting bored to death, out of the blue, we started talking about stars. I didn't care at all, but you wouldn't shut up. You loved the night sky so much. By the end of the night, you had convinced me of their beauty and the magic in their very existence. That's the day I'd reckon we actually became friends, but marriage? It wasn't even then.

A couple of years passed, and we dated different people, but you stayed my friend. And every time I would look at the night sky, I would think of your love for its stars.

It was when I had gone to Pune for my MBA. It was the first time I was living alone, and it terrified me. The night would terrify me. This one time the lights had gone out and the whole area was plunged into darkness. I thought, this is it: this is how I die. I closed my eyes and I thought of those stars and out of the blue, I asked you to remind me of their beauty to get through the night. And you did.

It wasn't even then, though.

After that, you would check up on me often and we started talking on video calls. Do you remember that? There were days I had nothing new to say, but you would just be on those Skype calls, so I was a little less alone. We would both go about our work, dusting, cleaning, cooking, and studying, with the call running on a stand on our desks. You were my only 3 a.m. friend ever.

It was your being there in the silence—That's when I knew.

And if you're wondering, yes, I always could tell how awkward you were with silence. It was hilarious. Actually, it still makes me laugh to think of it. But that's the point, I'm realising.

You really weren't great at it, but you were there.

I'm sorry to have hurt you—I know I have. I'm sorry I wasn't there for you the way you have been for me. You're a way better friend than I am. Always were. It's not an excuse, just a fact.

I'll explain everything else, should you want to listen. I will understand if you don't, though.

Either way, I'm carrying back a souvenir from Rishikesh for you.

Again, if you accept it of course.

Love,
Nanki

I attach a picture of the CD with the words scribbled on it: *'Let's fill our home with new music. A music of our own.'*

And send.

I stretch myself. My hands, legs, and neck. Change was exciting. To be anchored to just enough constants through the variables, even more so. I look at my phone. It was almost eleven p.m. I had yet another letter to go and no canvas for it yet. I look around my tent with fondness. Just as I was wrapping up for the day, my phone rang.

Rithvik. Within three minutes of me reaching out.

Oh, the relief. Whatever it was could be hashed out now. I was sure of it. As long as he was still around to ... whatever: listen, talk, yell, fight. He was here. I picked up, and his groggy face, with his messy hair, came on. It feels like coming home after a long, long day. For a whole five minutes, we both look at each other and say nothing.

"Hi," he finally relented.

"Hi," I whisper back.

Another few seconds of silence, and then, ever so softly, "I'm still that friend, you know. You just forgot."

"I know," I look down at my nails. It was hard to meet his eye.

"I'm clearly still not great at it, but I'll always show up, Nan. You just stopped asking me to."

If he said another word, I would have to cry, and I really didn't want to. I meet his eyes, buried under my apology. We had been kids back then and that had made it so much easier. At what point of adulthood—I think now—do we pick up the ridiculous notion that growing up meant not having to ask for help? When growing up is maybe learning how to ask it better, sooner, and even more fiercely. I looked at him, really looked at him and realised that growing in strength didn't need to take away from the beauty of vulnerability, that boundaries didn't need to be an electric fence. They could be a loving celebration too, to be shared with the ones who deserve the party. Ones like these.

"Stop seeing through me. I'm here. Is that enough?"

I nodded. It was more than enough. Above and beyond.

"... And what is this crappy music you have bought me?"

I laughed. "Oh, it's the best ..."

After a really, really long time, it feels like two old friends catching up on their lives till we drifted off to sleep with the call running through the night.

To me, we are the story of a love I was only seeing as it unfolded in front of me: the kind that flows with the determination of a river, accumulating within its folds all that changes and all that stays the same—even if it looked like a breaking down to build anew from. With its essence—a deep friendship—intact through it all.

Chapter 28

I was shuffling through my room in the early hours of my last day in Rishikesh.

It had come as an epiphany, the canvas for my letter to River.

The book! The very book I had been reading since the first day I arrived in Rishikesh, the one I had picked up from the little library on my campsite reception: the Bhagavad Gita.

I wonder how I hadn't thought of it before. I pick up the pen by my bedside table, flip open to the first blank page of the book and sit down to write:

'Dear River,

If the world crashes down, I'd want you to have this.

This book was written over ten thousand years ago. We hold it sacred and I see why now.

I read it on this trip and here's what I realised: even centuries later, we still ask the same questions of our existence:

Of Identity: Who I am

Of Purpose: Why I am

Of Direction: How to be, so I can be happy.

And in pursuit of those answers, we still always find ourselves standing at the brink of a waging war—only this time, the demons are within. And they're stronger than ever before. Want as you might, you can't turn your chariot and run away from the battlefield. The only way out is through.

Thank you for being the Krishna to my Arjun and helping me walk that one step further.

I am ready. I'm ready for what's to come. I'm ready to meet my fears. I'm ready to see God as they emerge through my faith in letting it go.

This walk down this path, that bridge—it is of courage.

I am ready for war. Let's see what this edge is about, shall we?

P.S. This is not a goodbye. This is an 'until we meet again'.

With Love—and forevermore,

A Liver.'

Yes. This was it—and now it was time.

It had been a forty-minute drive up to Mohanchatti—the village within Rishikesh popularised by housing India's most extreme Bungy. A beautiful winding drive up the mountains through the Lakshman Jhula, the beach camps, and the flowing river. I had kept my window rolled down to not miss a single frame of this heavenly landscape.

I had almost lost track of time when, with a jolt, I saw it—A road sign that announced: 'First View of Bridge: Jumpin Heights—the Bungy People.'

Here it was!!!

That place, straight out of an Instagram handbook of bucket lists. The massive yellow bridge jutting out—the one I remembered River jumping out of.

Whoa, India's most extreme Bungy indeed.

Oh, the stories it must hold.

As I arrive at the reception, I am whisked away to be briefed. My nerves are shooting through the roof. I can't spot River, so I assume that he's probably at the bridge.

After all the safety check-ins, it was time! I walk down to the bridge, a quick five-minute walk with the cantilever looming closer with every step, threatening... beckoning.

Not for the faint-hearted, her.

The glare from the sun blinded me temporarily when I noticed the familiar tall, rugged, and blue-eyed man walk up to me with a bounce in his feet to shake my hand. River met me at the foot of the bridge.

I instantly feel reassured.

"Finally! Welcome, Nanki," his accent was still disconcerting, but I knew from experience now that I'd get over it in a jiffy. What he had to say always overpowered how he said it, exotically distracting though it was.

"River!" I feel so happy to see him. I take my book out and hand it to him. My penultimate letter.

He stopped short, curious and flipped it open. When he looked up, I could tell he was touched.

"Not a goodbye," he read aloud, with a smile forming on his face.

"Not a goodbye", I repeated. "One last time, are you sure I can do this?"

"I got you here, didn't I? Trust me to take you through."

It's true, I would trust him with my life. And I literally was about to.

"Everything I've said so far is only my thoughts and my perspective. I hope you have thought deeply and have arrived here by virtue of your own choosing. Because beyond this point, the journey isn't easy. You will only make it through if it is genuinely your will to. I can only promise for it to be worth it."

I nodded.

"And if you have thought over it and arrived here of your choosing, then surrender to the process now and think no more. *This* is that point. The edge. If you decide to walk up to the edge, don't sabotage the experience by your fears. Let the experience take over. The more you think now, the less you will be able to act. This is that point where you get out of your own head and just live. Live the moment—it is yours. Less thinking, more feeling.

"Ready?"

I exhale with a forceful determination. I had decided.

"Take me to the end."

The edge is a scary place. In this case, it stood at eighty-three metres from the ground—roughly the equivalent of a twenty-five-storeyed building, with my ankles tied together, harnessed to a rubber cord, giving me the first full view of the depth of the fall.

It hits me with the full force of its magnanimity. My heart is banging against my chest. River was checking the cords. I blinked hard as I took in the landscape. A string of mountains jewelled the scene like jagged diamonds. In its midst, lay a wild forest patch. Serene, raw. The blurry mid-day sun cast a golden hue to everything it touched. There was a shallow tributary of the Ganga meandering through, gurgling below the cantilever just as one would expect her child to be: pristine, naive, and free. Then there was the edge. It brought me the chance to enjoy it all—almost to consume it—if I could only dare to take the jump. But it also showed me the depth I'd have to overcome to do it.

And because that mirrored the battle that I had silently been fighting within myself, I could neither bear to stay nor to look away.

"3…"

River yelled out his countdown, infusing me with the vigour of his command. "Spread your hands out wide, like the wings of an eagle…" River was right behind me, holding the back of my harness.

I close my eyes to brace myself. This was it. This was my moment.

"2…"

I open my eyes. Actually, I decided I wasn't going to miss it for the world. As I looked straight ahead, determined to surrender even through the jitters, I let myself feel.

It comes as a regular day, the extraordinary one.

Nothing about it is different, really—not the weather, not the people, not the life.

It isn't a storm, it isn't a whirlwind, it isn't a beginning, it isn't an end.

Just another day somewhere in the middle, but suddenly, the sun shines brighter, the wind feels like an adoring caress, and the day feels like a lover asking you to *dance*.

And you do.

I looked down the height, forcing myself to breathe.

It's just another day, but you're just wholly awake and utterly alive to it.

That's what an extraordinary day looks like.

"1 ..."

I unclench my fists and let the fig tree leaf be carried by the wind to my muse.

My final letter of love. To an eternal love: the mountains of Rishikesh.

It had scribbled in ink:

'You've seeped into me,
Like the salt swirling the depths of the Sea
So I don't even know,
How to let you go,
Because without you, you see,
I'll be empty of me.
—Never a goodbye.'

As it flies away from me, I imagine it persist through all hail and storm, just like my love for them. I could feel River inch closer. He looks at me while I feel a terrifying calm grip me as I hone in on my goal. I was going to conquer this. With the fierceness of a warrior opening battle, he whispered—"JUMP!"

Glossary

1. Aa gaya – has arrived.
2. Anardana – dried seeds of the pomegranate fruit.
3. Apna – mine.
4. Arre arre – an exclamation of alarm or dismay; like Uh-oh/ tch tch.
5. Bete – child.
6. Bhindi – ladies finger/okra vegetable.
7. Chaliye, shuru karte hain – Let's begin.
8. Dasvandh – one/tenth in Punjabi.
9. Dhaba aloo – A local preparation of potatoes.
10. Didi, sab theek hai? – sister, is everything okay?
11. Dil koi kamzor thodi hota hai. Itna bachaa ke chalegi toh sadd jayega! – the heart is not weak. If you save it so, it will rot!
12. Dosa – a thin savoury crepe, typically found in south indian cusiine.
13. Garma garam chai – piping hot tea.

14. Ghee laddoos – an Indian spherical dessert made in rich ghee.
15. Haan, haan bhaiya – yes, yes, brother.
16. Har har gange – an exclamation in praise of the river Ganga; All praise the Ganga!
17. Ja le aa – go, get it.
18. Jaaney tuuuu, yaa jaaney naaaa – whether you do, or don't know.
19. Jai siyaram – Praise Lord Ram!
20. Khaana – food.
21. Kirana – grocery store.
22. Kulhad – earthen cups, typically used for tea.
23. Namaste, suprabhat – Namaste, goodmorning.
24. Pooja bhandaar – the shop of religious supplies, typically used in hindu rituals.
25. Prana – life force.
26. Pranayama – breathwork.
27. Pundits – facilitators/scholars of hindu rituals.
28. Ram-phal – a fruit found typically in Rishikesh, named after Lord Ram.
29. Samosa – an Indian savoury deep fried snack.
30. Seva – service.
31. Tera mujhse hai pehele ka naata koi – You are linked to me since before this lifetime.
32. Yunhi nahi dil lubhaata koi … – One doesn't love just about anyone otherwise.

Songs mentioned in the book

1. Pal Pal Dil ke Paas by Kishore Kumar
2. Hanuman Chalisa by Shekhar Ravjiani
3. Tera Mujhse Hai Pehle Ka Naata Koi by Kishore Kumar

Acknowledgement

Whoever knew it takes a village and a half to put together rambles of thoughts into one cohesive story! After almost four years of pouring into this, of editors and beta readers and publishers joining the mix, I finally have something I loved. Had. Here on out, it is yours: The story, the characters, this journey.

Writing is neither linear nor pretty. But there are those that rub in neither and go about their days like you're not behaving like a zombie with a brain freeze. To my parents, you deserve all the credit for everything I will ever accomplish. You know my love of writing only exists because of your joy in reading it.

My editor, Dagny. Oh, you had me at hello. Literally! Our email exchange would probably deserve a book of its own. She did the unthinkable and made me fall in love with editors. Or maybe (and most likely) just with her. To have added so much to the book without changing a thing about my thoughts or my style of expression is some weird kind of magic.

Navya. The editor I didn't know I needed! Wanting the best for my characters and expecting the most out of them has made them come alive in a way I had always only ever hoped for.

To all the teachers that scribble little notes of encouragement in the margins of students' answer sheets—you may not know it, but you shape our dreams.

Finally, I have to thank my publisher, Nu Voice Press, for believing in me as a writer and becoming a team that bonded over a simple story of complicated emotions.